DELETE OFFENCE

By Dr Gershom Sikaala

DELETE OFFENCE

Dr. Gershom Sikaala

Digital Version

Digital & Print Copyright - Gershom Sikaala

First Publication October 2022

Publisher NewYox Media London

newyox.com

ISBNs:

978-1-64226-376-3 (Print)

978-1-64226-377-0 (Electronic)

www.gershomsikaala.org | gershomsikaala@me.com

Executive producer in Hollywood. His previous book "Look at God" was an Amazon #1bestseller. Founder of purekonect a new social media platform and global charity initiative. Founder of Hollywood Mastery Class in California; Zambikes International Business; His Presence Fire Ministries; United Nations Inter-faith Goodwill Ambassador; Awarded National Statesman.

Compilation and Typesetting: Adéle Visser of NobleLight Design & Publishing (South Africa) at visser969@gmail.com

Cover Design: Adam Engela (South Africa) at www.7genesis.co.za

Editing contributions: Morgan Nel of The Hedge Solutions (South Africa) at morgancnel@gmail.com

Global Sales & Dist: Newyox Media

Unless otherwise identified, all Scriptural quotations are taken from the Holy Bible: The New King James Version, The Amplified Version®, The Passion Translation and The Message Translation. Used by permission. All rights reserved.

Printed in USA, UK, Europe & Australia.

ENDORSEMENTS

Dr. Heidi Baker (Iris Global) - www.irisglobal.org:

"Gershom Sikaala is a dear brother in Christ, and I share his deep desire to see true unity growing throughout the whole church, between families and nations and peoples around the world. Every believer is a precious part of the Lord's inheritance, and we are made for one another. Gershom reminds us not only that offense, bitterness, and anger against our neighbors will always hinder our calling, but that it is in our daily, intimate walk with Jesus that we can always find grace to rise above these clouds and move into the peace that is beyond all understanding. I pray that Gershom's words will be a blessing to everyone who finds them, as Gershom himself has been a blessing to my family."

David Hairabedian (David Hairabedian Consulting) - Davidharbedian.com

*"Dr. Gershom Sikaala has done an excellent job again in his recent book, **Delete Offense!***

He clearly defines and exposes one of Satan's most deceptive tools that baits, hooks, and sinks many on their journey with Jesus; Offense. We are instructed, "do not be ignorant of the enemy's devices" (2 Corinthians 2:11).

Jesus told us that "It is impossible that no offenses should come, but woe to him through whom they do come! (Luke 17:1)

Be wise. Read this book. Delete offense. Walk out the blessing you were designed for in Jesus. It's time to live in the drama-free (and offense-free) zone with Holy Spirit!"

Joan Hunter (Evangelist / Author / Miracles Happen TV Host) - JoanHunter.org

"I feel it is impossible to overstate the need for a corporate revelatory experience concerning the spirit of offense in the body of Christ. This evil spirit is prominent, persistent, and almost everywhere. I am very excited about Dr. Gershom Sikaala's book Delete Offense. He has written a book that is timely, necessary, and vital for Christians to grasp in an age of entitlement and narcissism. It is not possible to walk in love with anyone while constantly harbouring offenses against them, which is why this book will be a life-changer for many believers. I highly recommend you read it and start applying its principles immediately. Get several copies for your staff and friends."

Chris Richie (Lead Pastor at Encounter Church Vegas) - Encounterlv.com:

"Gershom Sikaala has not only been one of the leading prophetic voices to the nations for many years, but he has also been an incredible friend and encourager to me and my family. I have been in the "trenches" with him on many occasions and I can tell you without reservation that Gershom lives an un-offendable life. He carries an authority from Heaven to release people into freedom from offense and bitterness. For anyone struggling to let go, this is a must-read!"

INTRODUCTION

Relational connection is a very powerful force in our lives. We were created for connection and all the blessings associated with that. Most of the time we live more self-aware and neglect truly knowing who we are partnering with and how it impacts our reality within the natural bonding processes over time.

This book is written to the believers in Christ, leaders of the Church and to everyone desiring to live abundantly in their relationships. We are becoming increasingly aware of the end-time signs in the words Jesus revealed in Matthew 24 sketching a vivid picture of what to expect in the last days. I sense the need to focus on relationships and what is causing the breakdown of such when God so intended us to live more abundantly in them. We need to prepare and know how to combat this force that threatens our unity in Christ.

Who we invest our time in is a powerful choice that determines the landscape of our lives. It will determine where we are going and where we arrive in life. It will impact our destiny and influence our purpose. Who we choose to be with determines both our temporal and eternal outcome. It is thus a vitally important subject for intentional contemplation, ongoing meditation, and specific strategy.

Since God is love, everything revolves around Him and this most precious and vital source of life. As growing believers and individuals, it is vital to intentionally develop our ability to learn to live and love like He does. Receiving the healing and wholeness of His love and "living water" on a consistent, regular basis allows us to in turn about, express authentic love, faithfulness, care and affection. Whether it be in family, friendships, romance, or our connection with God, cease this golden opportunity to be stretched and grown by His all-consuming love.

John 13:35 (NKJV)

"By this all will know that you are My disciples, if you have love for one another."

May you gain sound knowledge, apply the wisdom, and develop a humble listening inner ear or intuition so to be equipped to manage a vibrant, free and compassionate heart of love.

We ideally long for long-term, faithful, and fruitful relationships that bring significance and meaning in our lives. The hard work of bonding over days, months and years is worth the time and energy for therein we forge an immoveable support structure in raging storms, a solid foundation for wonderful living and unforgettable memories in our golden years.

Yet, most of us seem to struggle with the short-term fleeting friendships, the self-absorbed colleagues, and the distant family members. We develop resentment, bitterness and offense that hinders peace and pleasant purpose. When misunderstandings and prejudices tug at our bond, we too easily give up since confrontation is supposed to bring us closer together, not tear us apart.

These attitudes can especially become dangerous if we are not equipped to manage these times with the help of the Holy Spirit. May we cease to remain complacent, ignorant, or unaware of how healthy and strong bonds should form to benefit both parties.

Therefore, this writing aims to bring the light of hope through the truth of God's Word. If there is constant access to the highest wisdom available to us in the Bible, the Holy Spirit will illuminate and enhance our human intellect. We have the mind of Christ (1 Cor. 2:16) to build and accomplish far beyond our human capacities. Here is an example in Proverbs 24:3-6 (AMPC).

*"Through **skilful and godly Wisdom** is a house (a life, a home, a family) **built**, and by **understanding** it is **established** [on a sound and good foundation], and by **knowledge** shall its chambers [of every area] be filled with all **precious and pleasant riches**.*

*A **wise man** is strong and is better than a strong man, and a **man of knowledge increases and strengthens his power**. For by **wise counsel** you can wage your war, and in an **abundance of counsellors there is victory and safety**."*

Here we see the wisdom of the processes of relational structure. Using construction and warfare analogy we gain insight how to apply strong bonding in relationships.

This book on managing offenses will release keys how to choose and navigate in your bonding process in relationships, how to keep your spirit free and pure while you might be dealing with relational stresses. While you are forging new relationships, building lasting connections and managing break-ups in both long and short-term relationships, you can remain constant in the forming of your heart becoming like God's beautiful heart of love.

May we learn to truly know Him and be known by Him.

---- | | ----

Contents

Chapter 1

OFFENSE - THE END-TIME PERSPECTIVE

We live by God's amazing grace. His protection, provision and providence allow the believing heart to rise above and live abundantly in a broken and perverse world.

No one, however, is exempt of the temptation of living offended or being treated poorly by an offended person since lovelessness will increase. Yes, Jesus warned us that this behaviour will increase because of the intensity of issues growing in the world. Jesus said since rebellion and "lawlessness" (Matt. 24:12) will increase because of iniquities and sin, natural love and compassion in the world will also decrease.

Consider the prophetic season we are in, the timeline we are in in the powerful end-time words of Jesus in the Gospels. How privileged we are as God's children to be aware and prepared as worldwide offense increases! Let us look at Matthew 24:9-11 regarding offense.

*"Then they will deliver you up to tribulation and kill you, and you will be hated by all nations for My name's sake. And then **many will be offended**, will betray one another, and will hate one another. Then many false prophets will rise up and deceive many."*

These words might be true in your social media news feed or your television report but also might be affecting you personally. We thus accept that all people will have to deal with offense, betrayal, hatred, and deception in these times. It all depends on where you decide to place yourself in these times.

Will you live as an offended, grumpy negative person or will you live dependent upon Christ's love with joy, peace and be the solutionists for your generation?

Got Oil?

As mentioned in the introduction, wisdom is needed to build something lasting. As we live in the presence of the King, we become more like Him. Jesus' parable of the five wise virgins in Matthew 25 allows us to be prepared, matured and ready.

We can position ourselves according to how the Holy Spirit is corporately guiding and leading the corporate Body of believers in history. We see in these last years how the church is growing and getting ready by what the Apostle Paul laid out in Ephesians 4:10-13. The gifts of God were given to the Body for her equipping for the work of the ministry so that we are "built up". But this company of anointed believers must *unite* before we will reflect the mature image of Jesus. "At that time" speaks about the end-times ~ that time is now. This parable comes after the Matthew 24 description of what will happen at the end of days:

Matthew 25:1-3 (NIV):

"At that time the kingdom of heaven will be like ten virgins who took their lamps and went out to meet the bridegroom. Five of them were foolish and five were wise. The foolish ones took their lamps but did not take any oil with them."

The oil represents the abiding presence of Jesus. It is an oil joy Jesus represented while He modelled a Spirit-filled life on earth. He has transferred this oil by the Holy Spirit to every believer. It is resident in our spirits, we have the anointing of the Anointed One. We know we have been with Jesus when our joy remains replenished. We do not live in fear but in faith, ready to meet our Bridegroom at a day and hour that only the Father knows (Matt. 24:36).

Yet, there is no need for discouragement, anxiety, or fear. He promised to always be with us in our waiting and preparing. The oil of His presence, the oil of joy is what builds us up and keeps being replenished as we continually seek His face and walk humbly with Him. When Jesus spoke to the Samaritan woman at the well in John 4, He spoke of Himself as the "Living Water". It is the inexhaustible essence of His presence that will keep us strong, spiritually hydrated and loving when everything else is heading towards the grave. It is this joy within that can become depleted for it is meant to be so full, it is overflowing with His loving presence and therefore, also granting His wisdom to a broken world.

Since the disciples of Christ shall be known by this overflowing, life-giving love (John 13:35), submission and obedience to His authority will also increase. Spirit-filled believers will *"arise and shine"* (Isaiah 60:1) like those virgins with their lit lamps. In a darkening world the light of Christ's love will escalate and shine brightest. The authority over sickness, disease, wickedness, and the curse will disappear as we step into the fullness of His Spirit and use His weapons of overcoming effectively. Our submission and obedience to the voice of the Holy Spirit will bring about order in chaos and wisdom solutions in hopelessness.

Choosing to make His presence a priority in your life is not only going to grant you the wisdom for living and being discerning of the end-times but it will keep you offence-free in your relationships.

It is interesting that Jesus mentioned the virgins in plural – the virgins and not virgin. We get to do this together; we have no choice but to make sure we are in unity when the Bridegroom arrives. In the early Jewish tradition when a couple were betrothed to one another, the man subjects himself to his father who will observe, counsel and mentor him over a period. He will be required to get his house ready, his finance, his work ready so that the Bride can be received. Only the father can give permission for the wedding to take place. But to the bride is assigned virgin maids who help her stay ready. The Lord has so designed our safety, strength and the encouragement in numbers and togetherness when the world is dark and there is little courage.

Yet, the oil of the presence of Jesus will grant us the wisdom to be swayed or distracted by the needs of those who do not choose the replenishing presence of His love. Choosing the presence of Jesus above the presence of unwise friends takes courage for it can bring your betrayal, their offence and persecutory hatred from those you thought had the same focus as you do.

Our intimate life with the Lord is going to set us apart in wisdom. Those who do not choose an intimate relationship with God will be in the camp of the foolish and will remain in the bitterness and delay of offense.

If we remain focussed on the Bridegroom, we will not be distracted by those who have taken offence through their own negligence. We cannot foolishly give our oil away and lose our own salvation. The thief comes first to steal but he also comes to kill and destroy – the Greek and Aramaic text in the Passion Translation gives a more intense picture of what the enemy comes to do. To be robbed or stolen from is one thing but the ultimate aim is to "kill" which is translated as "slaughter" – a much more vivid picture of what kind of enemy we are dealing with and what he is attempting to accomplish in our lives and relationships.

John 10:10 (TPT):

"A thief has only one thing in mind—he wants to steal, slaughter, and destroy. But I have come to give you everything in abundance, more than you expect—life in its fullness until you overflow!

Everybody is going to hear the "midnight" cry on that day – everyone will know when it is the end whether we are in a state of wisdom or foolishness.

Will we be in abundance and overflow, or will we be in need and depleted? Will we be like those faithful priests of the tabernacle who heeded to the command to trim the lamps every day? Will we be willing to be checking our heart-lamps each day for His appearing and live distraction and addiction free? Will we allow our eyes to be taken off the Bridegroom by substituting Him for temporal relieving aids? Will we be heeding to our impulsivity, the carnal desires and motives of own lives, and be drawn away by the selfish needs and offense of those around us?

Matthew 25:6-10 (NIV):

"At midnight the cry rang out: 'Here's the bridegroom! Come out to meet him!' Then all the virgins woke up and trimmed their lamps. The foolish ones said to the wise, 'Give us some of your oil; our lamps are going out.' "'No,' they replied, 'there may not be enough for both us and you. Instead, go to those who sell oil and buy some for yourselves.' "But while they were on their way to buy the oil, the bridegroom arrived. The virgins who were ready went in with him to the wedding banquet. And the door was shut."

May the door never be shut to us. May we have the wisdom to tell the foolish ones to go and buy their own oil – to go back to Bible School to hear how to get their own relationship with God. Meanwhile, you remain positioned in worship and obedience at the treasure chest of His heart.

May you have the wisdom and the offense-free heart to keep your focus and soul replenished in these times when the devil is very aggressively stealing, killing and destroying. May you buy enough oil from Jesus each day and live and give in His abundance, to anticipate His coming and help those around you to do the same.

Proverbs 9:9-11 (NKJV):

"Give instruction to a wise man, and he will be still wiser;

Teach a just man, and he will increase in learning.

"The fear of the Lord is the beginning of wisdom,

And the knowledge of the Holy One is understanding.

For by me your days will be multiplied,

And years of life will be added to you."

---- | | ----

Chapter 2

BATTLING OFFENSE

The Year of War

We need to choose our battles wisely by considering what the outcome would be if we choose to either engage or not engage in the battle. As I see it, we have no choice as the kingdom of God is at hand providing the favourable outcome in the name of Jesus. In this year 2022, we have heard of wars and rumours of war in Ukraine which the passage in Matthew 24 also speaks about.

Nevertheless, not only is there a war in the natural but a war in the heavenlies in which we as believers need to be engaged in. Even though there might not be armies on our doorstep, we need to be aware that there are spiritual forces advancing closer to our spiritual territories that we need to defend and to fight against. Now is not the time for hiding behind a mask (Covid19), but to stand up in the power of the Holy Spirit and use our authority in Christ Jesus.

Now our generation and our children's children welfare are at stake. What will you do with what God has given you, equipped you with and who is currently in your life to serve this Kingdom first?

We know that life is a spiritual battle, especially when our unity and our love is being challenged in our close relationships. It is an indication that the enemy might have created a breach in our families, groups, fellowships, and churches what was meant to be unified and at peace. It is an urgent and present danger that we need to heed to right now and be adequately prepared.

There is however, not "a demon behind every tree", but there is a wise, Holy Spirit strategy for every situation and that is the wise solution from heaven for aspect of our lives.

Courageous Commanding Soldiers

As there are ranks in an army, we have also been ranked by the blood of Jesus to receive the authority by the Commander of Heaven's armies, our loving Heavenly Father to overthrow and overcome the enemy. When you stand in the confidence of your redemption and the covenant God has with you, all hell trembles at this authority. It is not because of you that they tremble but because of what God has invested in you.

He has provided the guidance and training by His awesome Holy Spirit to teach us to defend and fight in our spiritual warfare for spiritual and relational victory.

What's more we always have the intercessory prayers of Jesus in the heavenlies that "saves to the uttermost" (Heb. 7:25) those who depend on the Lord's highest rank in the heavens. By our covenant with Him, we have been spiritually seated with Christ in the highest heaven (third) heaven where we stand and overcome in His authority (Col. 3:1). He declared "it is finished" on the cross. We have the privilege of being under His command, simply enforcing that victory in the physical realm.

Prophesy Your Victory

The spiritual gifts of God are not only there to strengthen others, but they can be used to strengthen our own lives in God. After the description of God's love in 1 Corinthians 13, the Apostle Paul encourages us to desire spiritual gifts, one gift being above all ~ to *prophecy* as encouraged in 1 Cor. 14:1. If you need encouragement, go and prophetically encourage someone and see how quickly you come out of depression of negativity. The gifts should all be wrapped up in God's love for you personally. Prophecy is the utterance of His abiding love that encourages, comfort and edifies. This eternal love expressed from the heart is the fuel that grants us the courage to engage the battle and to endure the fight. You could even prophecy over your own life each day to comfort, encourage and edify your heart.

If you read through Ephesians, you will see the outcome of all God's gifts and equipping is for the unity of families and the body of Christ. This is so we may grow up and become mature unto the image of the Son. God has designed the victory to be a corporate one. Each one's dedication and engagement contribute to the whole. If we lack vision, we lack this ultimate purpose. If our vision is love and unity, we have the overcoming resurrection-life vision of the Christ in our consciousness. We will see healed and whole individuals and nations who desire to cooperate and build God's kingdom in a united, humble, and prayerful effort.

Encourage yourself in the Lord with Apostle Paul's words in Ephesians 6:10 (NKJV): *"Be strong in the Lord, and in the power of His might. Put on the full armour of God"*. By the indwelling Holy Spirit, you are covered by righteousness around your position in Christ; you have His truth around your identity as a child of God; you are shielded by your faith in what Christ has done for you; protected by the Word of God and your feet are purposed by the paths that God has laid out for you to follow.

A Chosen Vessel

Accept the fact that you were not only chosen to be a child and an overcomer in this world, but God has chosen you to be fruitful. You are the elect of God, chosen to be a carrier of His character and His purpose. You are an ambassador of the Most High God. Therefore, carry yourself with dignity and with humility. Know who you are in Christ for if you do not, the devil will continue plundering your life, home and work, coming to steal, kill and destroy while you have been given His royal life in abundance.

John 15:16 (Amp):

"You have not chosen Me, but I have chosen you and I have appointed you [I have planted you], that you might go and bear fruit and keep on bearing, and that your fruit may be lasting [that it may remain, abide], so that whatever you ask the Father in My Name [as presenting all that I Am], He may give it to you"

Not All Battles Are Yours

What God has assigned you to will have a victorious outcome since Jesus has already overcome on our behalf. Let us become sensitive and discerning in our intimate connection with the Holy Spirit to know what is invading our atmospheres and our emotional life.

Psalms 42:1 (NIV): *"Why so downcast my soul, put your trust in God!"* If you are achieving a favourable outcome in your business, you know that communicating to your boss and colleagues is part of the process to reach success. If you are aiming to bring loving discipline to your children, you would not think to not be communicating and talking with them often. Why do we thus neglect to keep speaking to ourselves and encouraging ourselves and others in the Lord?

As we are in constant bombardment each day and on

every level, His Kingdom wisdom is available, it is "at-hand" to position ourselves in assigned battles for our lives. We can get so caught up in every battle, we land up not having energy to fight and win the battles God has assigned to us. The battle or opposition coming against you is confronting your personal anointing, assignments and calling in the kingdom of God. It is personal. It is enforcing the redemptive dominion commissioned to us in the garden of Eden.

God has chosen you as His child and equipped you through His Word for every assignment and every battle that rages against you. Yet, most battles might feel personal but are against the anointing of the Anointed One within. Distraction and disguise are one of the major strategies of the enemy to be focussed on yourself. You might be in *the* battle of your life, but your mind is unrenewed or unaware of the urgency and strategy of the fight to bring about a kingdom victory. The Holy Spirit is at your right-hand – He is *the* counsel, protection and wisdom of heaven for your situation.

Receive the victory Jesus bought for you at His last words on the cross: "It is finished!" (John 19:30). He has completed and fulfilled the entire will of God on your behalf. He has given you the inheritance paid by blood to be reinstated to the Father's love and care. Now simply by faith in this mercy and lovingkindness, receive His strong empowerment to receive the truth and purity of His love for you. The opposition is the spirit of the Anti-Christ wanting to come against Jesus so arrogantly within.

Matthew 10:16 (AMPC):

Behold, I am sending you out like sheep in the midst of wolves; be wary and wise as serpents, and be innocent (harmless, guileless, and without falsity) as doves.

With the worldwide pandemic and the looming development of wars in the world this year, some of us are becoming more aware of how complacent and unengaged we have become because of the many changes we have been forced to accept and navigate through. We prophetically see the strategy of the enemy to keep us weak, unfocussed, compromising and discouraged amidst the call to rise and shine as true believers.

Disciples of Christ Disciple Others

The Apostle Paul used military analogy and language (Ephesians 6:11-18) to encourage **discipline** in the lives of believing families. He more than others from personal experience knew that should a single soldier be undisciplined, insubordinate, disobedient and unresponsive to the voice of the Commander, the strength of the whole army is weakened. Our daily submission and dedication to the Lord has great consequence on the Body of Christ.

This is a responsibility we need to accept with our salvation which needs to be *"worked out with reverend awe and trembling"* (Phil 2:12 AMPC).

The Classic Amplified translation expands this working concept as: *"self-distrust, with serious caution, tenderness of conscience, watchfulness against temptation, timidly shrinking from whatever might offend God and discredit the name of Christ."*

---- | | ----

Chapter 3

HOLY SPIRIT AND OFFENSE

With the powerful help of the Holy Spirit, we are enabled to do all things through Christ, but we need to be very aware of the responsibilities we have. This is since the Lord has granted us dominion in the earth. We still need to be prepared each day to exercise our authority and so bombard the gates of hell.

After a period of the disciples living with Jesus and Him imparting mindset, lifestyle and delegated authority to them, Jesus had to check whether they spiritually discern or know Him. He asked His disciples to confess their revelation of Him: *"Who do you say I am?"* (Matt.16:15). Imagine if we had to ask this question to the Lord and of ourselves each day? How different the outcome of that would be! In the language of governmental authority, Jesus said He gives us the "keys of the Kingdom" – the ability to lock/bind/disallow and to open/loose/allow. May we have that inner conviction to say "No, not on my watch!"' or "Be delivered in Jesus Name!" for the assigned battles God has given us.

Matthew 16:18 (NKJV):

"And I also say to you that you are Peter, and on this rock I will build My church, and the gates of Hades shall not prevail against it."

God Builds "In Secret"

Corrie Ten Boom wrote a book "The Secret Place" – a biography of how she supernaturally survived the holocaust of the Jewish nation in the last world war. It is a prophetic picture of what can happen when we live in the shelter of the Most High God. Even though all hell is breaking loose around us, those who trust in the Lord are sheltered and protected in His hiding place. They are at peace in the storm, they know that the number of their days are in the hands of the Almighty. Perfect love casts out all fear (1 John 4:18 NKJV).

When we know a storm is coming, we cannot stop what is going to happen but most likely empower and **brace ourselves in faith** working through love. We are prepared to stand against the natural forces and **position ourselves adequately** in advance in His spiritual forces. We cannot stop the effects of the storm, but we can govern our reactions to it so we may survive the storm, learn from it and execute the victorious command of God.

The Holy Spirit in An Army of Believers

Being prepared for something that can potentially harm is part of God's redemptive plan and will for each of us. Jesus said in John 14 that He has not left us as orphans (John 14:18), but He has provided His "right-hand man" – the Holy Spirit. In the language of a King, He is His personal representative that sticks close, as the "Counsellor". Among all His perfect attributes mentioned in John 14, He guides and leads us into all truth, buffeting and armouring us against the enemy's primary strategy: deception.

Having Holy Spirit counsel, therefore, is a battle strategy for the sons of God.

It is said of FEAR as an acronym: False Evidence Appearing Real. How do we discern the distractions and deceptions when innocents are being persecuted and hated for Christ's sake? How do we keep our focus on many who will forsake believing in Jesus, choose to betray and hate and take the path of offense? How will we stand against the false prophets that will rise up in these end-days? It is only by the Holy Spirit who is the Ultimate Genius, Flawless Counsellor and Compassionate Comforter that will lead us through. The Israelites were not diverted *past* the Red Sea, they were not led *away* from Jericho, He marched them *through*! And so, He will do for *you*!

It is in the *"secret place of the Most High"* (Psalm 91:1) that we will find this refuge and fortress. If you are in the company of *"the Most High"* you are also in an elevated position yourself. You are above and not beneath. Your altitude and attitude in Christ have already been established as the overcomer.

Be reminded that nothing can separate you from His love (Romans 8) and you are destined for the celebration of victory in every situation. When the battle is raging and there are so many voices of deception and distraction, the *"still small voice"* (1 Kings 19:12) of the Holy Spirit is your guiding force.

May you take your time with God each day as a vital need and necessity. Just like you would make an appointment with a CEO of a company or with your medical doctor, your time with Him as a child of God has a no-compromise focus.

In addition, Paul spoke practically about a mindset of *daily* resistance and positioning in the Secret Place of prayer: *"...standing; ...resisting; ...take up; ...cover..."* Prayer, as is praise and worship is our secret (stealth) weapon. It is no wonder that the first believers were called "disciples" – the word deriving from the "discipline". The five-fold ministry giftings of the Lord Jesus (Eph. 4:11-16) equips believers for the disciplined work of the ministry.

Being Under Command

I urgently appeal to every believer to engage personally with Holy Spirit today so He may reveal the Father's personal value of you – how He sees you personally. You need to *know* how you are equipped, what you are gifted in, *how* you are gifted and where you fit in the Body. In this equipping, He has also ranked you with certain authority by the price of obedience you have paid. Yet within that authority, you are a *servant* of all (Mark 9:35).

As mentioned in the previous chapter about the power of the unified virgins, God has revealed to us the power of servant-unity and so in this letter to the Ephesians, the Lord has given us the strategy to live an overcoming Christ-centred, unified existence with His Body. This is so the increase of unity with Him and others may result in: *"one Lord, one faith, one baptism; one God and Father of all, who is above all, and through all, and in you all."* (Eph. 5:5-6). The disciplined army of God is a unified and mature body of believers. Since not everyone professing to be in ministry are known by God (Matt. 7:23), choose your group wisely.

Believers who are constantly seeking the presence and prayer and praise is a priority. The church must return to making this the focus in ministry groups in this day.

Since such a high price of Jesus lifeblood was paid for each of us, granting us a covenant relationship with the Heavenly Father, it is our responsibility (response-ability) to adequately position ourselves in the body of believers who *are* disciplined leaders and *submit to* prayerful, humble, equipped, disciplined, and discipled leaders.

These are those who lives are surrendered to the Holy Spirit on daily prayer and obedience of the Word of

God. These are those who uncompromisingly demonstrate and teach the disciplines of Jesus from a heart of obedient love for Him. The neglect of this will increase the spirit of rebellion and subsequently offence and betrayal will cripple the momentum of the army of God.

Knowing The True Enemy

When Jesus was commissioning the disciples in Matthew 10:34-39 to go out and preach, He put out this caution as to who will be their enemies and who will be their alliances. He was preparing them for the resistance through deception.

A friend tells a personal story that you might relate to. He was friends with a believing family and shared most of his life with them, including some financial benefits. Due to the pandemic, business slowed down and when they were no longer gaining from him, he realised that friendship with him had taken a back seat. He felt used and abused and had to resist the temptation of allowing rejection and lies of the enemy to keep him stuck in his relational journey with God.

He had to decide to get off the fence of offence, surrender the situation in the hands of God to restore him financially and relationally. At least the situation had revealed the truth of heart motives and he could be more selective of his friends in future. When it seemed, there was no hope for some business dreams to transpire, they decided to part ways.

We must understand that no matter what spiritual level people may portray, there is always that human element of selfishness and greed when it comes to sharing business and finance.

1 Timothy 6:10 (NKJV):

*For the love of money is a root of all kinds of evil, for which some have strayed from the faith in their **greediness**, and* *pierced themselves through with many **sorrows**.*

When someone really values you, when people discern God inside you, it doesn't matter what happens or what gossip is spread about you. If they really love you, they will overlook sin and errors and respond in prayer and compassion. I'm not saying one must not be selective about friends. True love asks what can be done to sort out the problem together and tries to maintain the connection for the sake of kingdom purposes.

From Proverbs we find this wisdom:

Proverbs 10:12 (NKJV):

Hatred stirs up strife, but love covers all sins.

Proverbs 17:9 (NKJV):

He who covers a transgression seeks love, but he who repeats a matter separates friends.

When Offence Causes Rejection

Apart from Jesus Christ, the wisest man who ever lived, Solomon, said love is stronger than death. (S.O.S 8:6) - nothing should separate your heart from brother, sister, husband, or wife. If there's true love, there will not be a selfish agenda and love will rise above. If they walk away, they are also walking away from God inside you. You must make sure you are recovering and invest in your peace, in your own heart by receiving the counsel and healing available through Holy Spirit ministry through safe people in the Body of believers.

As you love God in all things, also love yourself knowing what your identity is based upon God's Word. If you carry offense, you will carry rejection and the enemy will be attracted to prey on your emotions and subsequent poor decisions. Choose to love and you will choose to heal and move on in life.

If you thought standing for the kingdom is just a peaceful protest of the enemy, readjust your attitude. Be prepared to meet combat in exercising your faith. We need to know what we have signed up to be and to do. He, however, is already the Victor within, as He said He has already overcome the world (John 16:33). Look at the opposition as you stand for God's ways.

Matthew 10:34-35 (NKJV):

"Do not think that I came to bring peace on earth. I did not come to bring peace but a sword. For I have come to 'set a man against his father, a daughter against her mother, and a daughter-in-law against her mother-in-law'; and 'a man's enemies will be those of his own household.'

Standing for the truth of the Gospel is going to bring division and it will bring offense. You need to accept this as a soldier of Christ, and God has provided the ways in which you can overcome and win the battle of offense. We cannot afford to be crippled by offence if someone rejects us because they are rejecting God within us.

Look at your heart and your dedication and passion for the King and His kingdom. Have a realistic view about who and what is in your way as you are taking up your cross to follow Jesus? These are not only your enemies but the enemies of the cross, the very source of your life and breath.

May your enemies not be those of your own household but here is the warning that it might just be they who oppose the purposes of God in your life. The love of the Father shown through the sacrifice of His Son on the cross is the love that will never leave or forsake, it is the love that trumps all other loves in your life – Matthew 10:37 (NKJV):

"He who loves father or mother more than Me is not worthy of Me. And he who loves son or daughter more than Me is not worthy of Me. And he who does not take his cross and follow after Me is not worthy of Me. He who finds his life will lose it, and he who loses his life for My sake will find it."

If we must lose relationships to gain Christ, we need to become resolute for it to be so. Jesus had a very realistic view of who were those opposing Him and who were aligning with Him. Those who are willing to be obedient, to follow God and do His will, no matter how difficult, are considered His family:

Matthew 12:50 (NKJV):

"For whoever does the will of My Father in heaven is My brother and sister and mother."

How Holy Spirit Heals

Words are as important as forgiveness is but to be made whole and to be really free of offence, we must come to a place of taking personal responsibility for both our words and the reactions to our words.

Once an offence is harboured, it creates a complex inner attachment to your life that grows when we allow it time. We must know and accept that the only certain thing in life is change. Growth and development are inevitable. Keep committing to the growth of your Christ-like character, not the growth of things that do not belong in your inner life.

The devastation on the disciples after Jesus' crucifixion left them shocked and traumatised. They had three years access to His personal presence, to His words and to everything He said He was going to do. There was this awkward in-between moment that was enclosing on their hearts and emotions, but Jesus suddenly transcended the walls of their hearts and home. He crashed into their fear and anxiety and proclaimed peace on the storm of their emotions. His immediate words were of purpose and destiny and then He enabled them to fulfil His words by breathing His breath over them.

John 20:21-23 (AMPC):

"Then Jesus said to them again, Peace to you! [Just] as the Father has sent Me forth, so I am sending you. And having said this, He breathed on them and said to them, Receive the Holy Spirit! [Now having received the Holy Spirit, and being led and directed by Him] if you forgive the sins of anyone, they are forgiven; if you retain the sins of anyone, they are retained."

This is a surprising scripture to me. One would think Jesus could be giving them all sorts of things in this moment, but He chose to give them the ability to forgive above all other gifts. Just like the Creator breathed life into Adam's nostrils at the beginning of time, Jesus is enabling us by breathing His life into our hearts right now. The ability to forgive allows us to live freely and creatively so we can get on with doing what He started and even greater things.

The breath of God starts repairing our innermost being. When your inner man is repaired, God's light will shine on the areas that need cleaning and healing. A wound always needs cleaning before it receives balm or a plaster. While you were experiencing the hurt and the pain, there was a lot of information your soul had built up. Since your soul and body are connected, that information could have negatively affected your body. Yet Jesus is the calmer of storms, and He is the Way-maker where things seem impossible to fix.

Receive the peace that He is still speaking over your life right now. Accept the calm and the rest that is in His voice and in His person. Invite the Holy Spirit in to clean your heart of the bitterness and poison vexing your soul. Allow Him then to heal those inner wounds, those words and actions that have cut and crippled you so deep that no psychologist or counsellor could help. The Holy Spirit's touch through His Word and presence goes deeper than you can imagine. He goes into your deepest parts to massage and soothe the bruising and detoxify you from the poison. He reaches into the depths of healing with a heavenly balm that penetrates and fills every aching part of our being. The anointing of His abiding presence is the oil of joy that brings that freshness, life and rejuvenation that brings about the resurrection life of Christ.

The Holy Spirit reminds us of the promises of God that were designed to bring us into rest. Not just when entering our "promised land" but while we are journeying there. While we are travelling through the various landscapes of life, we have one assurance that no matter what the terrain or the weather looks like, we have the Right Hand of God, the Holy Spirit taking us through, up and over. No one likes to be in the process of discipline or in the process of being in rehabilitation. But know that when we have been under the Potter's hand or the Surgeon's hand, we have been eternally touched by God for eternal change. The book of Hebrews describes this process as the Word of God working like a master surgeon:

"So then we must be eager to experience this faith-rest life, so that no one falls short by following the same pattern of doubt and unbelief.

For we have the living Word of God, which is full of energy, like a two-mouthed sword. It will even penetrate to the very core of our being where soul and spirit, bone and marrow meet! It interprets and reveals the true thoughts and secret motives of our hearts.

There is not one person who can hide their thoughts from God, for nothing that we do remains a secret, and nothing created is concealed, but everything is exposed and defenceless before his eyes, to whom we must render an account."
~ Hebrews 4:11

Maybe offence has been the means to expose your heart, to reveal your motives and a destructive secret thought life. It may be necessary so you may come to that place of freedom and unity with God. The Holy Spirit is the Wonderful Counsellor who leads you to become one with your Creator, closer to a holy God who is light and love.

---- | | ----

Chapter 4

THE ROOTS OF OFFENSE

AS we might relate, the disciples sensed a closing chapter approaching in their lives, so they questioned Jesus about the end-times. He so graciously started the prophetic discourse that was captured for our grace and blessings in these words from Matthew 24:4 (AMPC):

"...Be careful that no one misleads you [deceiving you and leading you into error]."

The Good Shepherd has foresight and foreknowledge and so we thankfully receive these words of warning and preparation. Part of our knowing Him is heeding His guidance about knowing our enemy. Our journey of conforming to His image not only remains in the daily secret place of His presence but it has an outflow, a fruit that grows which effects in our relationships while we mightily grow as warriors in Christ.

Offense is more harmful to the offended than the offender. We cannot underestimate the *"principalities, powers, rulers of the darkness of this age and spiritual hosts of wickedness in the heavenly places"* (Eph. 6:12). We are not fighting against flesh and blood, and we are not ignorant of the devices the enemy uses through the spirit of offense.

Therefore, when offence manifests, either internally or externally, we need to sound the alarm in the spirit. This we do by faith-filled prayer and declaration of God's Word and His promises. As we wait upon the Commander of the Army of Hosts in prayer and praise, He will grant us the insights and strategy against the manifestations. His angels are ready and waiting to partner with you with the word that God grants you in that moment.

Many times, the onslaughts are immediate and severe, so it is wise to remain vigilant and aware by constantly seeking our "right hand" the counsel and comfort of the Holy Spirit. As we pray in the Holy Spirit by "all manner of prayer", the Lord *is speaking, preparing and equipping us for every* moment of our day. As we are gaining spiritual fitness daily, the Holy Spirit will also prepare us for the day of His returning. Make sure you partner with watchful "virgins" of the Lord.

Ephesians 6:18 (NKJV):

"Praying always with all prayer and supplication in the Spirit, being watchful to this end with all perseverance and supplication for all the saints..."

Every Fruit Has A Root

Since Satan is the father of lies (John 8:44), he is always misleading, deceiving, planting error and hoping that we will place our trust in our limited intellect, proud opinions, self-centred mindset, or selfish logic. He is hoping that these thoughts and conversations with like-minded individuals who are submitted to demonic wisdom will affect our emotions and eventually settle our will to make an alliance with his corrupt ways.

2 Corinthians 2:11 (NKJV):

"…lest Satan should take advantage of us; for we are not ignorant of his devices."

The fruit of the Holy Spirit is the natural outflowing of His values and principles which comes from an abiding relationship with Father-God. One of these fruits is self-control and this is one of the foundations to decide to live apart from these habits that lead to offence. When our lives are rooted in God's love, the fruit of His presence will fulfil the full stature of the maturity of Christ within. It will bear fruit beyond our imagination and our generation.

When you are offended, you might have a relevant case to justify your offence. But the Counsellor, the Holy Spirit who has perfect judgement and foresight, goes beyond what is obvious and beyond what we cannot see. Logically, it looks fair for you to remain in your position, to hold a grudge but each day that passes keep you more deeply rooted in bitterness towards what someone said or did to you. But consider the Spirit-filled words about "demonic wisdom" (James 3:15) –

it *seems* wise, but it is cloaked, there is a hidden poison behind from a resident carnality, sensuality, and selfish ambition.

Nip the offence in the bud. Do not let offence or bitterness grow. Take immediate action with genuine repentance before God and humble apology at the appropriate time. In the context of not grieving the Holy Spirit, speak the truth, but do it in love. Keep unity and peace for that is where the Lord commands His blessing (Psalm 133). Living in peace with God means living in peace with God-fearing believers.

Ephesians 4:25-27 (NKJV):

Therefore, putting away lying, "Let each one of you speak truth with his neighbour," for we are members of one another. Be angry, and do not sin": do not let the sun go down on your wrath, nor give [a]place to the devil."

I pray God's wisdom when you must extend grace and forgive offenders who are not God-fearing. For in so doing, you "heap coals upon their heads" – God 's way re-ignites their dormant consciences and awareness of God's love and desire for them.

I pray that corrupt roots be exposed in thoughts, emotions, and intellect. May the pruning of the Lord be welcomed for whatever comes from His hand which always has blessing attached to it. Since His love is always the motive, He is always needing you to live, move and have your being closer to His heart and ways. May the desire for holiness be birthed in you as you read, meditate and pray about the things He needs to displace in your soul. May your heart be at attention, may your humble heart of worship and repentance grant you the courage to seek being conformed to His ways of living offense-free. He longs to occupy every room in your heart.

The Promised Land of Wisdom

From a prophetic perspective, we are reminded in the year specifically where God is training us in the perfections of wisdom. This is so we may be equipped to overcome and survive the challenges in this year and beyond. We need heavenly, supernatural wisdom since we have never been this way before. We can have all the experience, knowledge and all the resources in the world, but do we need heavenly wisdom, that which goes beyond logic, that which grants us the ability to apply the revelations He gives us.

In recent years, we have become aware of the increasing teaching from major spiritual leaders about the battlefield of the mind – the soul-realm with its strong will, volatile emotions and over-thinking intellect. The battle is to resist conforming to these ways of the world (Rom. 12:1-2).

The Word of God has a miraculous means to bring His wisdom to assist us to resist. This transforming force in the realm of the soul surrendered agrees with the ways of the Holy Spirit. With both the Word and the Spirit aligning in our hearts and minds, heaven and earth (spirit and soul) agree. With this united front, our bodies come in line with healing and strength and our world settles into God's promises. His wonderful blessings and abundance manifests as our "promised land" and our living becomes thriving and fruitful.

How do we distinguish between godly and human wisdom? We need to pray to be aligned to wise, godly mentors, counsellors and friends who live by the Spirit. Their godly advice, guidance and direction in these uncertain times is vital. Yet once again, the Champion Lion of Judah has overcome! He is the author of all perfect wisdom! True, heavenly wisdom has the attribute of meekness attached to it – it is selfless, humble, and loving. As we align our hearts with the easy and light yoke of Christ and we access the gifts of His Spirit through god-fearing friends and family, the good works He has planned for us, will grow.

James 3:13

"Who is wise and understanding among you? Let him show by good conduct that his works are done in the meekness of wisdom."

Synonyms of meekness: quiet; gentle; and easily imposed on; submissive. Antonyms of meekness are impatient, assertive, overbearing, just to name a few. Can we imagine our Jesus having these attributes?

Uprooting Offence

It is a natural process while forging relationships that soul-meets-soul when given the time. Time is how we bond – the glue, commitment, and faithfulness that wars against offence. Therefore, time and face-to-face fellowship should be approached as one of the most precious commodities in our lives and should be used and shared with intentionality and purpose. Our attitude and expenditure of time with God and with His beloveds determines the quality of our relationships.

In today's development of a technology-based way of communicating, people are becoming "virtual" to one another. The tone of voice, expressions of face and body language are becoming a lost art and people are losing touch with normal ways of conversing and communicating. It forms patterns in the brain that results in fruits of emotional distancing, unrelating to others and an unwillingness to bond and build together.

We must, more than ever, intentionally commit to avoid the conveniences of texting, voice notes and e-mailing in relationships that really matter and return to more meaningful and firmer bonding processes. There are obviously different approaches when it comes to the various relationships in our circle of friends, family and acquaintances.

The Psalmist wrote these contemplative words whilst in his season of being a forced vagabond. He made use of his offended heart during isolation to contemplate his worth to God and to himself. He also remained very wise about the way he wanted to respond about the injustice he was being handed out. He chose the path of wisdom concerning those who he thought were his friends:

Psalm 39:3-5 (AMPC):

"My heart was hot within me. While I was musing, the fire burned; then I spoke with my tongue:

*Lord, **make me to know my end** and **[to appreciate] the measure of my days**—what it is; let me know and realize how frail I am [how transient is my stay here].*

*Behold, You have made my days as [short as] handbreadths, and my lifetime is as nothing in Your sight. **Truly every man at his best is merely a breath!** Selah [pause, and think calmly of that]!"*

In addition, the Holy Spirit gave Moses, the humblest and one of the most mighty men of God, these words:

Psalm 90:12 (NKJV):

"So teach us to number our days, that we may gain a heart of wisdom."

I pray you allow the Lord to grant you an expanded, bigger picture of your life. I pray an orientation in your spirit-vision, that you will know where you are at in life and what your destination will be by God's grace.

God had anointed David as King, but a whole lot of people were not acknowledging or seeing the will of God. He had to remain faith-filled, faithful, determined and accepting of this anointing while the rebellious King Saul remained in power. It was God's means to show the nation that His choice is always best. Meantime, God preserved and graced David to learn the power of connection with Father-God while learning the art of bonding with the people He sends, for the purposes of God to take place. This however came from a willing heart, a heart that followed God's heart no matter what the cost. It was not only a means of survival, but it was a true living expression of worship.

Acts 13:21-23 (NKJV):

"And afterward they asked for a king; so God gave

> *them Saul the son of Kish, a man of the tribe of Benjamin,
> for forty years. And when He had removed him, He raised
> up for them David as king, to whom also He gave testimony
> and said, **'I have found David the son of Jesse, a man
> after My own heart, who will do all My will.'** From
> this man's seed, according to the promise, God raised up for
> Israel a Saviour—Jesus—"*

Through David's anointed life, we see a very long and painful process. May we learn to be spared from poor choices and bad bonding by not conforming to living after God's heart. There is no guarantee that anybody is exempt from crushing disappointment, emotional pain and heartache in relationships. Some started learning from a very young age and this world is a broken place but God has given us the Holy Spirit through the sacrifice of Jesus to have us overcome and gain the victory in this dark world.

After the gathering of rebels and outcasts at his hiding at the Cave of Adullam (2 Samuel 23), David realised that a new army of supporters was being given to him by God. They became known in history as "David's Mighty Men" and they left no stone unturned as recorded in the Bible of their mighty deeds. Yet, David had to be very careful how he would lead this band of robbers and vagabonds. He had to lean on the wisdom of the Lord to create a respect, discipline and a command in a group who probably had heathen background. He had to make sure they understood that his dedication and commitment was to God first and he insisted they conform to bow their knee to He who matters most. Considering their history of awesome military skill and passion, he could have landed up having to herd the proverbial cats but the wisdom in his heart through intimacy with God, set him apart as a leader of leaders. Even though he was surrounded by experts who could kill a person in many ways, their dedication to David (a supernatural intervention) found a will to risk their own lives for him.

However, David did something that would remove all offence or doubt that he was the chosen king of God. It came about, in that stronghold, when David expressed a longing to rest from Saul's pursuit, to have a drink of water from Bethlehem again. This sparked action (probably impulsive) from the dedicated soldiers wanting to prove their commitment and claim rank. The closest source of relief was in the Philistine's camp but that was no problem for these brave and accomplished men. The warriors risked their lives to bring David some water from the guarded well, but as he humbly received it from them, he poured it out on the ground as an offering to God with the words:

"Far be it from me, O Lord, that I should do this! Is this not the blood of the men who went in jeopardy of their lives?" Therefore he would not drink it."

2 Samuel 23:15-17.

Nothing could have prepared him (or them) for that moment of the precious water being spilled as an offering to God. This wise action coupled with these bold and genuine words, was not a contemplation and a pre-conceived notion. It was a reaction from a heart after God's own heart as a priority in His life. David knew how to gain the respect and the hearts of his followers, but he could have only done so by the supernatural wisdom of offering his own life as a love-offering before God.

When we are fully dedicated to God's heart, there will never be lasting offence, because your commitment to God cannot be contended or contested. May the love of God be so deeply rooted in our lives that nothing can uproot us from His will, not even the full dedication, love and commitment of the mightiest warrior in our midst.

We can learn from David about the royal mindset that He chose. He was always seeking God first in all things and it opened doors of favour but also of contention.

He decided to clothe Himself in the compassion, love and mercy of God and became such an example of true worship and a life dedicated. Jesus always had the approach of love in all He said and did.

May we clothe ourselves in the royal clothing of love and follow Him without hesitation and without compromise.

-

Colossians 3:12-14 (MSG):

"So, chosen by God for this new life of love, dress in the wardrobe God picked out for you: compassion, kindness, humility, quiet strength, discipline.

Be even-tempered, content with second place, quick to forgive an offense.

Forgive as quickly and completely as the Master forgave you. And regardless of what else you put on, wear love. It's your basic, all-purpose garment. Never be without it."

---- | | ----

Chapter 5

THE FRUITS OF OFFENSE

The Temptation of Offence

We must realise that every person, whether Christian or not, is going to be tempted by Satan through offence. When you say, "Jesus is Lord of my life!", the temptations of proving this the contrary will come your way. Accept that this is what you signed up for and you must master it. From the earliest days of time, God has been warning about temptation that waits like a stalking animal, waiting to pounce on the open opportunities we give it. These words were uttered to Cain when he was offended by his brother's favour with God and his offering being less accepted:

Genesis 4:7 (AMPC):

"If you do well [believing Me and doing what is acceptable and pleasing to Me], will you not be accepted? And if you do not do well [but ignore My instruction], sin crouches at your door; its desire is for you [to overpower you], but you must master it."."

See how the Lord was shedding light on his offence of his brother Abel? We have the awesome privilege of being accepted by Father-God by simply believing His ways are higher than ours.

Through our covenant with Jesus, we have acceptance

and access to the ways of the Holy Spirit set out by the example of Christ. Being under His love-command means we shall rule over temptation! Jesus proved this during His forty-day wilderness fast when Satan came with three major temptations (Matthew 4).

How gracious this prophecy is over Cain and even over each one of us. Believe the Lord – what is acceptable and pleasing to Him. Ignoring the Lord is being disobedient and rebellious which has consequences. We bring judgement upon ourselves. Remember from this account of Cain and Abel that God said sin and temptation have potential power to overpower us, but we only need to believe His words and follow His loving way. Choose this day who you will serve.

The Distraction of Offence

Now let me use an analogy from technology to strengthen my point. Some of you are aware of "notification settings" on your phone? There is a correlation on how temptation of offence comes to the way we receive daily notices on our phone. There is a way of programming your phone to allow you to see what messages or activity is happening on your apps. Once you've programmed this setting, you can expect to receive a sound, a vibration, or a text to remind you of calendar events or app activity. Although it is handy, it can become distracting at times. The key is you need to be selective by going through what is priority in your mind when programming the settings. You don't have to respond to every notification, but you can filter the bells, hearts, and checks so that at busy times, you're only checking what's important or a priority.

You have the inner filtering ability of the Holy Spirit to know: what is important; what is a distraction; what needs to receive action; what things can wait. Since the fellowship of the Lord is a light and easy burden, we should never feel overwhelmed or overworked. The meekness of submission to the Lord keeps us free from those traps that lead to things that aren't meant for us. If we however do step into those traps, we can ask for forgiveness and grace. Keep your relationships free of offence by managing priorities in this way.

Someone was planning an important trip, but while planning the details required, he received a distracting notification on his phone. It side-tracked his focus which caused him to leave out some crucial planning details. That one less important bell effected the way in which he got to his destination and the quality of his trip.

Similarly, we are challenged each day to better manage our focus. This enables us to develop a lifestyle, of not only handling all incoming communication or issues, but to learn to navigate priorities. The goal might be to become more efficient, not realising that that very means is a time-wasting temptation to satisfy curiosity. You could be determined, resolute and task-orientated in an assignment or goal but offence, grudges and even bitterness can distract and slow you down. It alters your focus. Just like those pesky notification bells. So much more reason to be in constant synergy with heaven throughout the day so you may have that higher vantage point of seeing, knowing, and walking in the Holy Spirit. The Lord lives light-years ahead of us. He is surely Master of Technology.

At one time, I was invited to attend a very important event in Hollywood. I was supposed to go to the host's party which allowed me to make imperative connections. (As a minister, I have a principle that if you're not networking, you're not working.) For some reason, during this time, I was so offended about something that happened and I decided not to go to the party.

I regretted this decision later and realised I could have

met some very famous people. I had missed an opportunity to minister to people who would not in any other way have heard about Jesus and the gospel of salvation. They had missed out on the evidence of His love and His power. It is not about fame and money; it is about the priceless value of the soul.

I was so grieved about this missed opportunity, but I learned a very expensive lesson: that anger and offence can distract you from a moment in time ordained by God for you. It can divert you from an eternal assignment that can mean the eternal life and death of a soul. It cannot be taken back, or it may not come around again.

Your calling and purpose need to be above any emotional or hurtful things caused by offence. The focus is not about people's opinions or criticisms, it is about getting the job done that God requires of you. You need to remain faithful and focused on Jesus in times when you are especially emotionally challenged. Sometimes, one must ignore offence in order to stay focused on obeying God. It will enable you to keep your job or to be effective in the workplace.

What is your mission and your goal? Do not focus on blame and injustice. God created you with a divine purpose – it is beyond your emotional needs. You are bigger than situations because you are the child of God. There is no demon that you cannot cast out, no obstacle that you cannot overcome or mountain you cannot climb. Your only limitation is allowing offence to grow root in your heart and control your life. Do not let the poison of offence grow in your life but allow God's wisdom to grow. Do not lean on your own understanding but pray for insight, knowledge, and wisdom. Learn from the situation and let everything turn into kindness and love. Let everything you go through push you to move forward.

The Procrastination of Offence

There is a difference in being a spiritual person and being a person without principles. That is the reason why many spiritual people are poor. As a believer in Christ, you are invited to choose to also be a disciple or follower of His ways. If you determine to be disciplined by the Holy Spirit to follow the principles of Christ, you will be wealthy. That is His will. The disciplined sons of God are those who truly belong to the Father. They have the character and substance to bring solutions to the world.

Wealth will be attracted to you, but you must look after your heart, especially the emotional and physical places where you were hurt. Also, be kind to yourself as a ministry to God. Look after your body, watch what you eat. He is the Good Shepherd leading you to those pastures green where you are totally healed and nurtured. You only have one life, one body, one mind with one mission to please your Creator.

Therefore, do not worry about what people think of you, but what God thinks of you. Take time to read His word – study God's thoughts and ways. Know the plans He has for you (Jer. 29:11-12). You are not an accident; you are also not a mystery. Whatever you go through, it is because you were thought worthy to experience it and grow from it. You are greater and bigger than trials and temptations and God trusts you to overcome it. He has placed things in you by the power of the Holy Spirit which allows you to grow and thrive. You do not constantly have to be in a fight for survival – there are times He wants to comfort and strengthen you with leisure times in the presence of family and friends ~ even spiritual family who love you like their own.

Psalm 91:16 (NKJV):

"With long life I will satisfy him, and show him My salvation."

Some of you have been fighting for yourself all your life. It is time to surrender to the Lord, to collaborate with Him in His destiny for you. Find out who God is and so find out who you are. What is your Jesus-mission?

When people remember you, what do they think about? In one sentence, what will you be known for? There are certain people in history whose story might fascinate you. I think of the inspirational lives of Kathryn Kuhlman or Ralph Wilkerson. There is a reason why we are attracted to their biographies. It might be because their past echoes our future and contributes as an encouragement to what we are becoming in God.

Work on yourself and find that specific purpose that will bless others. Your life will be filled with peace and joy, not just happiness. As for me, I love to bring God's solutions into seemingly impossible situations. I love to pray and hear from God to bring healing, restoration, and encouragement through Word of God and through the gift of prophecy. I also love to walk in wisdom to counsel and mentor people. These are my passions and I realise this is how God created me – to be a world-changer and a problem-solver. I've created various companies that have brought about technology solutions. Do not be afraid to step into the unknown if you have given your plans to Him. He will change and help you achieve the goals you submit to Him as your leader and finisher or your faith.

Proverbs 16:9 (NKJV):

"A man's heart plans his way, but the Lord directs his steps."

Psalm 139: 16 (NKJV):

*"Your eyes saw my substance, being yet unformed.
And in Your book they all were written,
The days fashioned for me,
When as yet there were none of them."*

The Delay of Offence

Often, when we get offended, we feel we want to quit. Life doesn't have to stop there. Most people do not really care about your offence. Anger and frustration – yes those are real feelings, but life does not stop for you to allow you to stay in your pouting bubble, licking your wounds or remaining in this self-focussing, distracted and isolated position.

What has worked for me? I just allow myself to breathe. For a moment, I'm thankful for being alive and release grateful praise for the grace of being brought to this point. I just breathe in and breathe out three times and let the situation go into the hands of God. I ask the Holy Spirit (my Helper and Best Friend) to counsel and assist me in the process. We must understand that human beings are inherently selfish and do not care about another's inner processes as they are dealing with their own mess. What we cannot see is that which is underlying, emotional and of the mind, is *your* battle and *your* issue. But it should never be a lonely or isolated position to be in.

In the past when I was offended, all my energy went into trying to get over the offence by either logic or will. These thoughts would steal hours away from the wisdom received from reading the Bible or being innovative, or having solutions, spending time to win relationships. Now I've learned to ask myself: "How can you use your time in a better way?"

The Wilderness of Offence

Life is like sowing seeds – what you put in the ground will come up and germinate as the rain hits the good soil. Life is a culmination and a partnership with things we control (mortal) and things we cannot control (divine). The seed is destined to germinate but if it's in the wrong environment and there is no rain, its potential is lost. Offence is like that dry or barren ground that disallows the seed to break through and sprout. If you hold a grudge, hold your anger, it is like forgetting to plant your seed. But as you keep watering your seed by optimism, goodness, forgiveness and surrender to God's healing strength, you are keeping your heart-ground clean and most of all, providing yourself that environment for your life to keep advancing and flourishing despite the offence.

The biggest lie the enemy has been using, is that you can "take your time", it is "okay to not be okay" (for long periods of time), "it is what it is." All these statements are partial truths that feed destructive procrastination and delay coming into your own and into a greater rhythm of being a "life-giving" spirit.

1 Corinthians 15:45 (AMPC):

Thus, it is written, The first man Adam became a living being (an individual personality); the last Adam (Christ) became a life-giving Spirit [restoring the dead to life].

The Isolation of Offence

It is said that money can be reprinted, but time cannot be remade. If it's in your means and time, give life, speak life and walk into life today. "*Sufficient for each is its own trouble.*" (Matt. 6:37) Build those relationships and that life-dream and pray for grace to partner with God so you may accomplish what's been given in your hand for that day. Obedience is the test of love. God is our source, and He loves to enable us to remain faithful and focussed on the dream He has placed in our hearts. Notice the words "trust", "delight" and "commit" in the following scripture:

Psalm 37:3-5 (AMPC):

Trust *(lean on, rely on, and be confident) in the Lord and do good; so shall you dwell in the land and feed surely on His* *faithfulness, and truly you shall be fed.*

Delight *yourself also in the Lord, and He will give you the desires and secret petitions of your heart.*

Commit *your way to the Lord [roll and repose each care of your load on Him]; trust (lean on, rely on, and be confident) also in Him and He will bring it to pass.*

Time does not wait but offence can hinder you moving forward. Emotions are real but these need to be surrendered to the Lord in prayer so He may work with your heart and character in the process. Place the offence in an imaginary box and give it to Jesus ~ let Him work a heart-miracle for you. Do not take back what has already been given to Him. He destroyed your offense through His sacrifice on the cross. Do not allow the anger and bitterness to hold you back from advancing through the lesson of offence and becoming Christ-like and mature in your walk of life. He is coming back for a mature, spotless bride.

Things are not always as you want them to be. Thriving does not always mean you're in a perfect environment. A scripture says of Jesus being as a tender plant which grew roots in dry ground (Is. 53:2). Your emotions or over-thinking wanting to create that diversion of bitterness, should not interfere with your will to do God's will. God designed you with a free will. Do not listen to the enemy to give up this freedom but keep choosing life despite what your head and emotions are saying.

Once you decide to focus on remembering what God thinks of you, what He promised you, being positively productive, your language starts changing, your conversations are focussed and very soon, your emotions will line up with the will of God. You enter back into that eternal zone of grace beyond earthly and temporal influences.

---- | | ----

Chapter 6

OFFENSE IN THE CHURCH

THE very place where there is supposed to be peace and safety has become an open door to the enemy. There are many churches worldwide but are they all true churches being built on the Rock of Christ? Churches built on intimacy with God has a wonderful unifying, coercive effect on relationships. One might be able to measure our unity and relationship with God by how unified and peaceful our relationships are in our gatherings and fellowships.

Yet from experience, there seems to be so much offence in churches it is withholding people from the best God has for them. I sometimes ask myself why religious structures hold so much hurt when it is supposed to hold so much of God's love! Why are so many churches, belief systems and ways of seeking God harbouring offence among leaders, pastors and priests?

The problem with this is not so much the issues that divide but that people are blindly following these so-called leaders. Not every person is called of God or is from God (Matthew 7:22-24). The Holy Spirit grants us His discernment as to know if a person is truly submitted to the Lord and committed and called for Kingdom purposes or not.

The Deception of Cultish Leadership

The reason why we shouldn't be offended when we are rejected or persecuted by spiritual leaders is because there is freedom in truth (John 8:32). This truth of God produces light that pierces the darkness around it, and it makes the opposition feel uncomfortable or threatened. So, you are shining God's light and you are just too bright for their liking.

Whilst you are being used of God to reveal the secrets of people's hearts (probably unknowingly), His light is binding the cultish spirit which is controlling everything. The Lordship of Jesus is not "lording over people" but a servant's heart of love. The Apostle Peter encourages sound leadership in the church:

I Peter 5: 2-4 (NKJV):

*Shepherd the flock of God which is among you, serving as overseers, not by compulsion but willingly, not for dishonest gain but eagerly; **nor as being lords over those entrusted to you,** but being examples to the flock; and when the Chief Shepherd appears, you will receive the crown of glory that does not fade away.*

Notice the emphasis here is on servant leadership. There is a difference between dictatorship and oversight. There is a difference between compulsive actions and Spirit-guided leadership. There is a difference between unwilling and willing hearts in leadership. Working for God is not about monetary gain, but about gaining trust. It is a sense of holy awe and fear in being accountable to the Lord for those souls entrusted to the leaders. Where there is this kind of leadership, there is no space for offence.

Offence-Free Leadership

A true spiritual leader called by God is not supposed to bind you but liberate you. He is not supposed to be a controller but a server. He is to be under God's love which leads his flock into the greater freedom of their God-given vision, dream, and destiny.

This liberty enables you to be creative, to develop and grow, walking in the joy of your anointing and calling. He comes along you in prayerful relationship to help and support you to become everything God created you to be. It is recognizing what God has put in you, protecting that gift and being an activator of that gift.

The religious ("Pharisaic") or cultish leaders who have an incessant need to control are not really interested in your development but are simply waiting for your fall. The type of leadership modelled by Jesus, was a leadership of freedom. Even when Jesus wanted to heal a person, He never imposed Himself on the person. In Luke 18:35-43 Jesus met a beggar near Jericho who was blind for most of his life. The man's need for healing was obvious, yet Jesus respected his will. He activated his faith by asking him what he needed Him to do for him. No matter how much compassion Jesus had, if the man did not confess his need, Jesus could not work with unbelief and the man would have remained blind.

We look at the willingness of the disciples who followed Jesus. He approached them with an intentional invitation leaving them to hear the voice of God for themselves. Sometimes, He used prophetic insight to convince them of their need to follow Him, but they were still given the freedom to stay or leave.

Tension or conflict is inevitable in every relationship, and it is most unlikely that you will have a flawless relationship with your spiritual leader. It is however during these times that we need to be especially vigilant of any control or manipulation while issues are being confronted and hopefully, resolved. Be prayerfully aware that you may also be tempted to force situations, be impatient or insist on having things your way. But since the goal is unity and peace, allow the Holy Spirit's work behind the scenes through your surrendered prayers. Without your presence or words, He will guide you when to speak up and when to be silent. Through your focus on His word and ways, your thoughts will begin to gather, and wisdom will come according to God's word. As you wait upon Him, avoid any carnal influences to govern your thoughts, words and actions. At the right time, you will be guided and directed to specific actions. Only be willing to be obedient no matter the outcome.

A cultic leader who feels threatened by truth will not only shun you. but try and cut off every relationship you have in common with him. Even if you're not directly related to the conflict, the spirit of cultism will try and isolate you to seize and maintain full control.

A true leader will surely protect his members, but he will respond in love when there is conflict. He will always keep an open hand with relationships you have in common and will not slander or spread the issue to others in your social circle. It is not uncommon that there could be disagreement but there should always be that regard or respect for each of us being sons and daughters of the Living God. Reconciliation and forgiveness work through true spiritual leaders but cultism wants to destroy you, your name and your relationships.

Sometimes people get so offended by religious spirits they end up never going back to church. The problem with this is not with your pastor or leader but with you not heeding to the guiding voice of the Lord in the first place. Get the truth and confirmation about your calling for yourself through pastors, leaders and mentors and position yourself accordingly.

The challenge is choosing the right people to stand around you. You will know a true mentor when someone is genuinely interested in your personal life, character, personality, gift and purpose. They are not only interested in what you can *do* for them or *give* them but in *you* as a person and a child of God.

Discerning True Leadership Without Offence

You need to be aware of the lifestyle of a potential mentor – does he or she really live in submission to the Lordship of Jesus in their lives? Can you really see the love of God or are they just duty or leadership-driven? Do you see the spirit of forgiveness and repentance, and do you sense the love of God? Does he or she feed on the love and presence of God rather than on their own personal agenda and ego?

Discern a cult or a Jesus-culture. Never make an enemy, rather avoid or run away from cultish behaviour. God has a kingdom plan and purpose for every believer, and He wants you to be connected to an appropriate, equipped leader to help you fulfil the kingdom vision God has given you.

Leaders must equip you to be focused on God and encourage you to be both intimate and obedient to the Lord. The five-fold ministry giftings of the Holy Spirit mentioned Ephesians 4 are there to build you up not break you down. There should not be a clashing or stepping-upon the gift God has given you. It is there so that you can reach a corporate unity with the Body of Christ. Jesus is returning for a pure and mature bride. Believers are to unify in maturity and so reach the full stature and measure of Christ (see Eph. 4:7; 13).

It is so important that we discern and recognize spirits that are not from the Lord but are used by the enemy to bring distraction and division to God's kingdom. Some of these leaders have a form of godliness but deny it's power (see 2 Tim. 3:1-5). Paul commanded Timothy and his followers to turn away from such people. Leaders sometimes tolerate and allow people to stay in the company of believers. These are people who have not been sent by God or who have proven themselves over time to live contradictory to the love and principles Jesus laid down for us. A little leaven effects the whole

(Gal. 5:9). Some of them might even walk in miracles, but Jesus will turn these people away for He does not know them (Matt.7:21-23).

Many have encountered such a person and most do not have the courage to confront them, so they are tolerated. Yet our courage to do difficult things is given by the Holy Spirit. If He guides you to leave, do not just disappear but make an appointment to respectfully speak the truth in love. The aim is for them to see the light, to restore them, to lead them to repentance keeping watch over your own heart in the process. We are called to bear and share the burdens of those who are in error.

If they cannot confirm their calling from God or if they are teaching erroneous teachings and do not want to repent, you should disconnect from them. Make sure that you are aligning with God personally concerning your own calling and doctrine. You cannot break connection without a sound reason and an intentional meeting. The teaching of Jesus in Matthew 18:15-19 concerning reconciling a relationship that has been affected by sin must always be regarded.

If they are called of God, but control and manipulation is the sin, very clear reference to sound and Biblical reference is to be made. This is a very intentional and prayerful process, and it requires bringing in trusted and very wise counsel to assist you to bring repentance and reconciliation. That is why you need to invest in lifelong trusted and mature leaders who are available to you assist with this by the Holy Spirit's wisdom:

In Matthew 18:15-19 Jesus clearly explains the outcome in relational tension ~ it must be repentance towards agreement. If two agree and are in unity, prayers will become a powerful, authoritative force. How interesting it is that Jesus gave the following instruction in the context of relational reconciliation. We are using our authority in prayer to bind and loose – not in a manipulative, selfish way but in the freedom of that which God has commission you to do. Abuse will not reach you unless you allow it. Discern the motives behind actions and God will show you how to pray by agreeing with what Jesus is already praying for you. Be careful of soulish prayers out of bitterness, hurt, anger or fear. These prayers are powerless.

Even Paul recognised people who were against him, yet they were uncompromisingly confronted with the truth in love. Paul suffered much for the new covenant we have today in Christ. He gained his rank and authority by the maturity and wisdom in his tenacity and focus to follow Christ without offence. Many so-called believers were lovingly confronted because their motives were corrupted.

The spirit of offense is connected to **religiosity**, and it effects so many social structures, even in the workplace. As soon as you receive the compassion of the Lord for your offenders through your intercession and prayer for their souls, God will do His work and you will have His testimony of how He has intervened and brought peace that transcends logic.

Know that the only true and perfect leader is Jesus Christ. He modelled the perfect ways and character of the Father and so when we keep our eyes on Him, our disappointments will not fester into offense and bitterness. We can give the offenders over to God in forgiveness and grace, knowing that you are able to forgive with the same forgiveness God has extended to you. Jesus breathed on the disciples (John 20:22) after His resurrection and said with this impartation, they will be enabled to truly forgive. It is His work through us maintaining a lifestyle of peace and healing.

Always compare your sufferings, rejections and persecutions to what Jesus had to suffer for us. It brings perspective, comfort and strategy to painful relational processes in friendships, families and the church.

Hebrews 12:1-3 (MSG):

Do you see what this means—all these pioneers who blazed the way, all these veterans cheering us on? It means we'd better get on with it. Strip down, start running—and never quit! No extra spiritual fat, no parasitic sins.

Keep your eyes on Jesus, who both began and finished this race we're in. Study how he did it. **Because he never lost sight of where he was headed**—*that exhilarating finish in and with God—he could put up with anything along the way: Cross, shame, whatever.*

And now he's there, in the place of honour, right alongside God. When you find yourselves flagging in your faith, go over that story again, item by item, that long litany of hostility he ploughed through. That will shoot adrenaline into your souls!

The Easy and Light Yoke of Offence-Free Ministry

When Jesus commissioned His disciples, He knew He was giving them a heavy responsibility. Yet, He gave a solution and a provision against fatigue, persecution, and discouragement. He said "Come to Me" in Matthew 11:28 *and, "Take My yoke upon you and learn from Me, for I am gentle and lowly in heart, and you will find rest for your souls. For My yoke is easy and My burden is light."* "Gentle" in this scripture is also translated "meek".

May we become the meekness, patience, and gentleness of Christ, yet being under His command. May we come to the root of our offences because of this attribute that the Holy Spirit is helping us engage in.

Jesus warned to expect to engage in this battle of deception of the wrong kind of wisdom. All the gifts and attributes of God are wrapped in love and there is no "shadow of turning" in this regard.

James 1:17 (NKJV):

"Every good gift and every perfect gift is from above, and comes down from the Father of lights, with whom there is no variation or shadow of turning."

Again, here we see how God has provided for us to know what is of the tree of the Knowledge-of-Good-and-Evil and what is of the Tree-of-Life. We are still being required to choose right, to use our will to the glory of God yet this time, we are being aided by the precious Holy Spirit who never leaves or forsakes us.

Humility Looks Good On You

When meeting Heidi Baker, you realise that her defining attribute is humility. It is a door leading people to restoration. Humility looks good on every person, no matter where they come from. Her submission to and love for the Lord brings a conviction and a humility in the awareness of His presence.

I was spending time recently with Heidi who has been ministering in Mozambique for many years. In contrast to ministering to the poor and destitute in an African country, I asked her the question as to why in a first world country, there is so much division and contamination of true faith within the Church.

If we all begin to acknowledge each other's grace giftings and each person is edifying one another and not destroying, there can be unity and strength restored.

The purity of Christianity comes through Jesus Christ alone, through the Holy Spirit. The mixture of faith brings a distorted perspective of one another. So, we need to lay down our egos and humble ourselves so that He may be exalted.

Humility is acknowledging who you are and who your brother is. It is from this appreciation that a gift to make new friendships and building bridges starts to work in and outside of church. Humility always makes you win. Mother Theresa was a very good example of humility.

Proverbs 22:4 (AMP):

"The reward of humility and the reverent and worshipful fear of the Lord is riches and honour and life."

---- | | ----

Chapter 7

AN OFFENSE-FREE WORK-PLACE

THE success of a business is not only measured by who is in charge but by the rate of happiness and work ethic shown by the general staff of a company. You can be the catalyst of a happy atmosphere in your home, workplace, or school by remaining offense-free.

I was once introduced to the mayor of a city as a spiritual support and advisor. When I was invited as a guest to a meeting, I was encouraged to open the meeting with a word of prayer. The mayor seemed to be such a good person and we enjoyed his charismatic personality as he shared about his plans for the city. I thought of introducing him to a friend who would be interested to fund his endeavours.

But some events took place which revealed what was truly going on in the mayor's office - behind the smiles and the warm welcome. As we were going to another meeting, I made the effort to greet the mayor's assistant. I was surprised when she suddenly and for no reason rudely dismissed me from the building. Maybe my prayer caused an offense in her heart? What could have been a great experience and an advantage to the mayor's office was doused with the negative attitude of the assistant.

Later, as I travelled with the wealthy woman wanting to donate to the mayor, she asked my advice about writing a check to him. I placed her attention on the animosity of his assistant. I shared my doubts whether the mayor was truly the person he was presenting himself to be since his assistant was showing such bad character. I asked her whether she wanted to invest in the values and principles that the mayor represented through the poor attitude displayed by the assistant. Without hesitation, she changed her mind. She wanted to stand for Godly business dealings.

I've been blessed this way in many relationships. One time I visited a friend many years ago. They are very wealthy people. They asked me what I thought about a certain man running for president. Little did I know that they would go on to donate $5 million towards his campaign because of my favourable comment. As leaders, we must be careful who we are surrounding ourselves with and take accountability of the words we exchange.

Your attitude determines your altitude. Favourable gestures and friendliness open doors. Kindness and mannerly connections keep the atmosphere offense-free, an atmosphere encouraging communication and favour.

On another occasion, a wealthy friend had it in his heart to invest in my ministry, but he wasn't telling me about it. He was seeking God about his decision so he invited me for one night to a very prestigious hotel so he could be undistracted in discussions and prayer. We were received with so much grace by the hotel staff and every effort was made for us to feel welcomed and cared for.

He asked for my opinion about the hotel and its service, and I expressed favour. He so regarded my opinion; he extended the one-night stay to a further four nights. Should the hotel not have had the right management in place giving the support staff such great work ethic, they would have lost out on an extended booking.

Our personal lives are like a business. The way you respond to people will receive a response in return. How people pay you back is through your attitudes and so it worth being mindful of your thoughts and attitude. You are like a business, forget about the structure. The business is you, so if you want to make revenue or income and live happy in life, it is rooted in your exchanges - how you treat yourself and others.

There's one restaurant I go to here in Beverley Hills. It is just a simple place, but I love it so much, I have made it a regular meeting place for friends. The manager and waitresses are so friendly and efficient. I have been tipping the waitresses well, but I always grant the one waiter an extra tip for his great work ethic. His respect and honour are so refreshing, and I have even considered to bless him more.

Creating Your Workspace

Develop a heart of kindness and prepare your workplace and atmosphere to be clean, clear of clutter which supports and speaks for you. It is very important to have a positive outlook in your workplace.

Even consider your workplace as an extended space of your home. Just like you would decorate your home, you can create an environment where it is uplifting and encouraging. I have found such joy in having pictures up describing who I am which bring gladness to my heart and others. I have photographs of places, people and events that bring memories of joy. They remind me of people who are closely connected to me spiritually and this supports my identity and values.

Skill and professionalism are so important but there are people who will enjoy greater success because they exude considerateness. They genuinely care for people and invest in good relational connections. Avoiding little offenses in the workplace will result in a stress-free, positive environment.

We are indeed blessed to be a blessing. Everything we do must become acts of worship to the Lord. As we determine to seek His kingdom first, may He grant that all our needs be met. The following scripture from the Message Translation says it so well. How we are to conduct ourselves in the workplace to honour God as we work and build relationships.

Hebrews 13:16 (MSG):

"Make sure you don't take things for granted and go slack in working for the common good; share what you have with others. God takes particular pleasure in acts of worship — a different kind of "sacrifice" — that take place in kitchen and workplace and on the streets.

As was mentioned at the beginning of the book about the perspective of offense in the end times, may this book and scriptures encourage you to continue being a good steward of your heart and life. May you live free of offense, deleting it from your life allowing the Holy Spirit to occupy every room of our hearts. It is a contagious state of being.

Matthew 24:45-51 (MSG):

"Who here qualifies for the job of overseeing the kitchen? A person the Master can depend on to feed the workers on time each day. Someone the Master can drop in on unannounced and always find him doing his job. A God-blessed man or woman, I tell you. It won't be long before the Master will put this person in charge of the whole operation.

But if that person only looks out for himself, and the minute the Master is away does what he pleases — abusing the help and throwing drunken parties for his friends — the Master

is going to show up when he least expects it, and it won't be
pretty. He'll end up in the dump with the hypocrites, out in
the cold shivering, teeth chattering."

Ask Yourself Some Real Questions

When you're going through a problem, take time to
calmly pray and to think. So doing, you may be given
the ten steps required to stay ahead of your enemy and
attacker. The mind is a golden place to bring salvation
to your current situation or future problems. But when
you function out of anger and offence, you may never
see the light for you will be lost in the darkness of anger and offence. You will even find yourself regressing
deeper into problems.

Ask yourself why you were offended and why the
person offended you? You must understand we live in
a fallen world. You must come out of denial at these
times to accept the reality of what the situation is truly
all about. Some people's hearts can be deeply wicked
and twisted. But don't let a heart of judgement allow
you to fall into the same trap of becoming twisted. You
must keep your heart and mind clear and ask the Holy
Spirit to minister to you in the situation.

Scriptures instruct us not to conform to the world's
ways - where dog eats dog and retaliating out of judgement as at the order of the day. Think twice before suing
a fellow believer and follow the protocols of approaching the person in person from Jesus' words Matthew
18:15-20 first:

"Moreover if your brother sins against you, go and tell him
his fault between you and him alone. If he hears you, you
have gained your brother. But if he will not hear, take with
you one or two more, that 'by the mouth of two or three
witnesses every word may be established.' And if he refuses
to hear them, tell it to the church. But if he refuses even to

hear the church, let him be to you like a heathen and a tax collector.

"Assuredly, I say to you, whatever you bind on earth will be bound in heaven, and whatever you loose on earth will be loosed in heaven.

"Again[d] I say to you that if two of you agree on earth concerning anything that they ask, it will be done for them by My Father in heaven. [20] *For where two or three are gathered together in My name, I am there in the midst of them."*

Use the protection and security structures laid out by the Lord. Should this method not be submitted to by the offender, it is permitted to separate yourself from such a person as they are in rebellion towards the protection of the Lord when sin is committed among believers. This passage particularly gives this command in the context of believers to remain in agreement so that our authority in Christ is not hindered.

Alternatively, it might be a workplace situation where authorities are involved and so you might have to get in the experts or lawyers in to help you. Through it all, keep your heart pure and keep yourself free of offense. Delete the offense! In doing so, you are allowing divine power to intervene on your behalf.

---- | | ----

"

Chapter 8

RELEASING OFFENSE

Take Courage

One of the ways we remain mediocre in life is to keep complaining and rehearsing who did whatever to us. No matter the extent of hurt, betrayal, or slander by friends and even family, you must accept and expect that you are not exempt from these experiences. In prayer, you receive the courage of the Lord to remain dependent on God to exercise forgiveness and the overcoming power of His Spirit for every challenge.

You have no choice, there is only one remedy in these cases ~ the partnership you extend to the precious and faithful Holy Spirit. His truth will always trump and protect you from a bad situation becoming a curse which in turn may develop into all kinds of mental, emotional, and physical effects should you allow it.

Jesus had this mind about the enemy: He did not only resist the devil, but He insisted he be forbidden to have any effect in His life. Jesus gave us power to allow and disallow things and upon this concept, God advances the kingdom of God through us. When you are being tempted, tried or tested, don't just stand there, place yourself in Christ and do something about it!

Matthew 16:19 (AMPC):

"I will give you the keys of the kingdom of heaven; and whatever you bind (declare to be improper and unlawful) on earth must be what is already bound in heaven; and whatever you loose (declare lawful) on earth must be what is already loosed in heaven."

Jesus countered Satan's advances by wielding the powerful Word of God. Jesus knew the mind of the Father for His life, and He simply applied it to the temptations and trials coming to His life. He walked in the fullness of the Spirit's power. He, being the Son of God, was not exempt from these challenges and therefore, neither are we.

Get up and make the decision to take the victory Jesus has conquered for you. Not everything will be perfect, but God is the perfect One who is always with you. Take the courage to step out in His presence and step into what He has placed in your heart. You can expect resistance from the enemy and even from people, but you can remain unshakeable in His love.

Spend time in the Word and in prayer and start writing down the ideas that come to you. Recognize which ones are from God by the "inner witness" of the Holy Spirit, for they will dramatically alter, improve, and change your life. Not everyone will agree with your ideas for they might have personal motives that are not always in God's thoughts. Know that you are a solutionist in this world so do not be distracted by the diversions of offence.

Remember Who You Are

The power of remembering what Jesus has freed you from and provided for you, will break you into a new day – away from the substitutes, addictions and crushing condemnation, even trying to constantly make-up for something in guilt that has already been fixed and forgiven by your Father. The saying must be repeated: "Let go and let God".

Before the cripple was healed, Jesus said to the man who was lying on his mat for most of his life: *"…pick up your bed…"* (Matt.9:6). That mat represented the lifestyle he had become used to, the attachment of his disability to the home he had fashioned for himself, the acceptance of his condition. Part of the man accepting the healing power of Jesus was to transition his thoughts, expectations and lifestyle into the normality and healing that Jesus was calling him to live in.

Sometimes we are hanging on our sins that are already forgiven, the past, the betrayals and offences that happened many years ago. We are allowing them to stay in our blood and our emotions. We need to take the hand of Jesus, "pick up that mat" and walk out of that sickness, pain and embrace forgiveness and life.

I remember once my friends and I wanted to drive out into Orange County and wake up early to watch the sunrise. We so enjoyed the beauty and splendour of that sunrise. Jesus is like that sunrise; He is the light in our dark world. You might be enjoying the heat of the sun daily, and one takes that for granted but the value and beauty of the sun is sometimes only realised when quietly sitting down, taking a breath watching a spectacular sunrise or sunset. Are you enjoying the blessing of the Lord, but have forgotten His beauty? You can be enjoying the blessing of the Lord to live life, but sometimes you must pause to worship Him and investigate His light to appreciate the fullness of Who He is in your life. Our minds can be full of the Word, but our hearts can be cold and callous. He came to illuminate mankind like the sun illuminates the universe.

Without Him, we form our own destructive thoughts and opinions, our choices are governed by our emotions and desires which lead to a dead-end street.

Do not focus on the darkness of the past but focus on the light. Our eyes were meant to operate with light streaming through them, not to focus on the night. Many times, we are fascinated by the stars, the moon and even flashes of lightning, but those are momentary experiences that cannot be compared to the exuberance and reality of life where everything is bright, positive, illuminated and revealed by the life and grace of God within.

I have regrets in life – things I wanted to do and didn't do, things I wanted to invest in which I didn't invest in. But I refuse to live in this limbo. *Today* is full of life and opportunity and I focus upon that.

Deny Impulse

I was watching the Oscars this year and a certain couple became controversial news due to a certain seasoned actor slapping a comedian on stage who made an insulting statement about his wife. The offence taken about the comedian's comment caused the actor to be banned from attending the Oscars. He forfeited acclamations in the industry for the rest of his career.

We can learn from this incident that one can never afford to be impulsively reactional, no matter how well it is justified in the moment. There is always another side of the story, no matter your point of view. That is why Jesus commanded us not to judge (Matt. 7:1) for it is not only about right or wrong. Only He has the capacity to give perfect judgement. If we give judgement over to Him, we will be exempted of being judged in return. This is trust, this is faith in God who can turn an impossible situation into a blessing.

We can never react on emotions, but only respond upon the principles we live and govern our lives by. Jesus said that how you see life is how you are going to react without giving much thought. Your heart's condition and intention are either shaped by God or by His enemy. Every action has a reaction and most of the time, and sadly so, it also effects our environment and innocent relationships. We always pay a higher price for choosing reaction above response. It will prove to reveal a broader ripple effect in time – more than what we think within the moment.

It is interesting to note that there has been report of the said actor apologising to the comedian. Unfortunately, that was not emphasised, only the negative was spotlighted. Isn't that how our human nature harbours bitterness and offence? By not focussing on what good came of the incident and the insult?

Forgiveness is not optional but a vital necessity. Should unforgiveness continue to be a prideful, stubborn choice? Matthew 18:31 to 35 warns us in the Parable of the Unforgiving Servant, that the torturous outcome is clear:

"So when his fellow servants saw what had been done, they were very grieved, and came and told their master all that had been done. Then his master, after he had called him, said to him, 'You wicked servant! I forgave you all that debt because you begged me. Should you not also have had compassion on your fellow servant, just as I had pity on you?' And his master was angry, and delivered him to the torturers until he should pay all that was due to him.

"So My heavenly Father also will do to you if each of you, from his heart, does not forgive his brother his trespasses."

Release Ego and Selfishness

One of the keys to overcome offence is learning to give our ego and self-centeredness to the Lord and allow Him to permanently deal with it. He has already overcome all things on the cross of His covenant with you.

The prerequisite is to follow Christ and to let go of what society dictates, what your preconceived ideas are, what you think is convenient for you and to conform and cling to His ways.

Matthew 16:24 (AMPC):

"Then Jesus said to His disciples, if anyone desires to be My disciple, let him deny himself [disregard, lose sight of, and forget himself and his own interests] and take up his cross and follow Me [cleave steadfastly to Me, conform wholly to My example in living and, if need be, in dying, also]."

Understand that there is no such thing as "a greater man or woman" for what is born of spirit will bring life and growth but what is born of the flesh will bring death (John 3:6). Those who have received the Holy Spirit, who are spiritually born again have already received the most honour, favour and greatness. In addition, you have been given the ability to be transformed into the likeness of Jesus. We thus become great when we begin to abide in Him and tap into the abilities of God within us. We realise that our talents and achievements are not our own but that they are from God's partnership in our lives. By grace we are gifted to be and to do – understand that our dependence upon Him requires a thankful life of humility and a grace to walk in fear with Him.

Isaiah 57:15 (NKJV):

"For thus says the High and Lofty One Who inhabits eternity, whose name is Holy: "I dwell in the high and holy place, with him who has a contrite and humble spirit, to revive the spirit of the humble, And to revive the heart of the contrite ones.""

Pride is exhausting, but humility is refreshing. It is like allowing foreign or corrupt matter into your digestive system and bloodstream. Dealing with offence is like food poisoning to your soul or like ingesting a deadly poison that will prohibit you from advancing and succeeding. The anointing and presence of Jesus displaces pride to humility. He desires full occupation of His person and His Word in our lives. As we commit to loving obedience, all His promises and wealth flood into our lives.

Release Bloodline Offence

Sometimes offence is a generational thing that can be passed on from one generation to another. We do not have to belong to offence or to grudges. We must free ourselves and come in holy alignment with God. Just like you would take your car for an alignment check, so we need to align our soul to the ways of the Lord. When a vehicle has completed an alignment, is travels smoother, saves fuel and safety features are more effective in an automatic car.

Similarly, coming into alignment with God, increases your protection and makes your life smoother and faster. And just like the alignment check of your car, your life will increase in longevity. You must come into agreement with yourself and with God that you will not waste your life and time on offence. I am not discounting valid thoughts and emotions, but we need to come to a place where we are not reacting emotionally but responding maturely to the ways of God. If you've committed a sin against God, your conscience will convict you. But as soon as you cry out to God, you are acknowledging your need for forgiveness, and your guilt will be released.

If you've been dealing with ongoing issues for a long time and you do come to a time of deliverance, you might still struggle with emotions that make you believe you still have an attachment to that sin. Know that you do not need yet another deliverance session but a complete overhaul of your belief system.

John 8:36 (NKJV):

"Therefore if the Son makes you free, you shall be free indeed."

You *are* free, you *are* forgiven and that settles it. Therefore, you can move forward right now. Human sin does have long-term effects and consequences on our bodies and emotions, but we need to encourage ourselves by faith with the truths of the Word of God.

I have found that there are righteous and good people, but they still live in condemnation and in guilt of their past. Even though the Lord has freed them, it is like a person being a slave for many years. The habit of consciousness will linger until an intentional end is made to it. This also works in the confusion of love and abuse – many are used to abuse because they have translated it as love. We must vehemently adopt living in the truth of God's love and His forgiveness. He is the Healer, but we are to receive and appropriate that healing for ourselves so that our minds and bodies are living free from the chains of the past.

Release Offence With God's Word

One of the paths to healing is to speak to your body, for there is power in your tongue using the Words of God.

Proverbs 18:21 (AMPC):

"Death and life are in the power of the tongue, and they who indulge in it shall eat the fruit of it [for death or life]."

Tell your body you are free, tell yourself you have been forgiven. It is similar when it comes to healing – you must be in agreement with healing and not with pain.

Job 22:28 (AMPC):

"You shall also decide and decree a thing, and it shall be established for you; and the light [of God's favour] shall shine upon your ways."

So, if you want to remove limitations in every area of your life, you must start receiving the thoughts of abundance, not poverty, increase and not decrease. Decree them into your life so they may manifest.

Believe To Become

There are various spiritual dimensions, and the Lord wants us to grow and mature in the fullness of what He designed. You can advance in different spheres like: forgiveness of sin; financial prosperity; spiritual gifts in operation; living in health; healthy relationships. But for all of these to manifest, we must mature in our belief system. We must access these, and we have to unlock ourselves to the Lord, so to receive them from our generous heavenly Father.

Water and fire can cook food but if you don't know how to use these elements, they can be harmful to you. Even having access to water and fire is part of a blessed life, in Mark 9:22 it tells that there was a demoniac who constantly harassed a man by using these very elements. Many times, the things that are supposed to be beneficial, are corrupted to be used by the enemy if we allow him. The enemy may convince you that that which was meant for blessing is now part of what you must accept. You deserve to be tortured or discomforted, but the power of the Blood of Christ is greater than this.

Learn to enjoy life when you have received the deliverance, freedom, and blessing from the Lord. We have been given both blessings and boundaries and with that, certain things that we are not to follow and submit ourselves to. Sometimes the world will teach you vengeance and revenge are the only way. But Romans 12:19 says:

"Beloved, do not avenge yourselves, but rather give place to wrath; for it is written, "Vengeance is Mine, I will repay," says the Lord."

We must give God room for the things that belong to Him and for the things only He can do. We are to submit ourselves to these words and keep our egos in check, telling ourselves we are nothing without Jesus. He is the only One who makes us somebody. With His strength and power, we are built up, not destroyed.

It's my prayer that you will come to forgive your parents, exes and leaders who have done you wrong so that you can have a healthy lifestyle and live in the overcoming power God ordained for you. You must choose His way, to love at all costs, because offence can rob you of sleep, keep you in depression and disallow you to enjoy life, even the simplest things in life.

Live your life off-the-fence – free from offence, in peace, joy and forgiveness. Let go of that fence, stop leaning on it and embrace your now and your future. Let go of the past and enjoy your new day, not your yesterday. Enjoy *this* day! Step into a new you – change your mind and accept your freedom by the Blood of the Lamb. Your work and your ways are going to improve. Tell your heart to beat again and your body to be free again, that is going to be healed. Tell your mind to be free of negativity. Learn to disconnect yourself from negative influences and the broken past.

Delete Your Offence

To "delete" seems to be both simple yet very difficult. It is the same word used in technology - to "trash something" or delete something from the computer. The word simply means to cut off something or let it go.

Letting go is actually one of the most difficult things, especially when you have the guilt of your past or the offence of others over many years.

Here's the thing, the fact that you're alive is God's permission for you to overcome offence. The only thing that is keeping your from letting go is unforgiveness. The longer you hang onto offense the longer it will cause unforgiveness to build up.

You might have an issue with your parents, pastor or family. I do relate since I had an issue with a pastor and with people that I grew up with. But the way I got through it was to let go and to forgive. You might be holding back something but know that your spirit is not breathing. You are too concerned about your emotions. Rather focus on the fact that you need to be free. Your emotions are a blessing, but it can be a curse at the same time, if you do not take control of your emotions. It doesn't mean you are to supress or ignore your emotions, for your emotions are a blessing from God to bring healing to your soul. But you cannot allow it to overtake your life.

Find God's words and promises that will begin to feed your starved soul and grant you eternal substance to live by - the abundance Jesus promised in John 10:10.

When there were angry words, you felt rejected or were made to feel inferior; someone belittled, misused and used you. Find the loving and reassuring words of the Father who never leaves nor forsakes you. Any person, despite how you were raised, has been subject to some of kind of abuse or trauma that has caused you to hold on to the offense. It is time to delete this and start living.

Look at Jesus' foundation – He lived in total freedom. He even forgave the criminals' words, while He was in excruciating pain, on the cross. Your offence might seem like your crucifixion but allow the breath of God to fill you right now, so you are able to forgive just like

Jesus did. Hesitation to forgive is like choosing to crucify yourself and remaining to hang between heaven and earth. It is choosing to remain in the realm of death on not embracing life and moving on. Release the debt to the Lord by saying "they know not what they are doing". That is how Jesus completed His life-task to become the Saviour of the world. Forgive so you might be forgiven by God in return.

Matthew 6:14-16 (AMPC):

"For if you forgive people their trespasses [their reckless and wilful sins, leaving them, letting them go, and giving up resentment], your heavenly Father will also forgive you.

But if you do not forgive others their trespasses [their reckless and wilful sins, leaving them, letting them go, and giving up resentment], neither will your Father forgive you your trespasses."

Luke 23:33-34 (AMPC):

"And when they came to the place which is called The Skull [Latin: Calvary; Hebrew: Golgotha], there they crucified Him, and [along with] the criminals, one on the right and one on the left.

And Jesus prayed, Father, forgive them, for they know not what they do. And they divided His garments and distributed them by casting lots for them."

Matthew 6:30-33 (MSG):

"If God gives such attention to the appearance of *wildflowers—most of which are never even seen—don't you think he'll attend to you, take pride in you, do his best for you?*

What I'm trying to do here is to get you to relax, to not be so preoccupied with getting, so you can respond to God's giving.

People who don't know God and the way he works fuss over these things, but you know both God and how he works. Steep your life in God-reality, God-initiative, God-provisions. Don't worry about missing out. You'll find all your everyday human concerns will be met.

---- | | ----

Chapter 9

MOVING FORWARD

I never thought I would become a speaker, like I am today. I started out as a young man, just sharing my experiences with the Lord from Bible readings and prayer. While reading the Bible I simply started underlining words that touched me because I was curious. This consistent habit is how I received my wisdom and the way I see life today.

Since the age of 14, I found such refuge in the Bible. Now that I live in America, I'm grateful for how God has led me to the company of Godly people who mentored and cared for me ~ specifically a mothering figure who would invite me to come and speak.

On another day I came in touch with an amazing mentor. He had a group called "Brave Mentorship" – it cost bravery to be mentored. He walked and talked with me. He taught me a lot about being humble and teachable and how to mentor others.

One day he told me about a meeting he wanted me to attend, and he introduced me to a powerful man of

God and his precious daughter. On a certain day, we were visiting Disney Land together. This was especially a wonderful experience for me since I was not exposed to things like these as a child. So, this experience and our connection bonded us in a special way, and we continued to keep in touch.

On another occasion, the husband and I were together again at Disney Land but to my surprise, he was confronted by an agent of the court who served him divorce papers from his wife. He was devastated to learn that he was also evicted from his home in the process and so he turned to me for refuge. I gladly offered my home as a solution for him, but it did not come without a price.

From that day, all ministry and business opportunities started drying up. Clearly, there were details about his life I was unaware of. I had not realised that my invitation of sharing my personal space with him had created such a huge offence. Furthermore, the offences and burdens that he had been carrying, was also coming upon me. People were disapproving that he was sharing my home, but I had no choice to help someone who was stranded. I had gotten to know him as an honourable person and that was who I was choosing to focus on. I had not known what had transpired in the past.

Then there were people who I thought were God-fearing who started slandering me because of my connection with him. I continued the noble stance of honouring my word to help my friend out, despite their choices that contradict my conviction to help him. It was very disturbing as I regarded them highly. To my mind they were like angels and powerful representatives of God's kingdom. How could they do something like this to me?

Then I asked the Lord about it, and He guided me to let them go and to release the offence. I received immediate peace and calm about the situation. My emotions were no longer troubled, and my mind was thinking straight. One moment I was in the dark and the next moment, the healing and freeing light of God was showered over me. I was innocent in this case, but they were treating me as guilty and an accomplice of whatever he had caused towards them. I could've stayed upset, angry and felt like the whole world was against me. But I was simply going to delete the offense, I was going to release the trigger or the trap that was holding me back from growing, learning and living.

Power To Move Forward

You always need to mind your own business; find your own business; find your purpose; find those things that align with your dreams. Do not give in, because someone is offended, or someone does not like you. Do not give in because you feel like you've lost their support.

When you persist and remain consistent, that is what defines you, that is what makes you different. Different is very often being in the opposite spirit of the world; the conformity that withholds you from moving forward. People will respect you, as they will know that you really know what you are doing ~ you mean business over what you represent. You have not given up, but you have kept your eye on the purpose. You have avoided being angry - which is wasting your time. You have focused on what is important, you have kept going back to the basics. You have even redeemed the time because of being upset. Things have you failed to achieve because you have developed anxieties through the offence.

You must learn to control your impulses and your emotions and know that everything you go through is temporary. What really matters is your future, your dream. Your future is like taking care and nurturing a baby – keeping it from any danger. Anxieties and depression are the things that will withhold you to grow and develop the roots of God's love in your life. Avoid living in limbo and in delay.

I pray you will receive the power to let go, move on and to move forward. God is light and light photons are always on the move. They are never dormant. God's seed within is always growing and bearing fruit for His glory.

Keep Your Heart Pure

Proverbs 4:23 (NKJV):

"Guard your heart above all else, for it determines the course of your life."

While you are dealing with issues, your heart might be experiencing excruciating discomfort and pain beyond description. Especially when you must deal with the anger that rises because of offense. But if we keep offense and anger for too long, it builds a nest and then it will breed more bitterness.

This makes me think of the time I was given an opportunity to visit someone's farm while the usual occupants were away for a week or two. We were not aware that the fridge was turned off and that the meat was busy rotting inside. As we entered the house, the smell permeated the entire atmosphere, and the odour was almost unbearable to endure. The house was very clean, but the smell made us oblivious to the pleasant interior. Fortunately, we eventually figured out that the smell was emanating from the fridge, and we removed the rotting contents. Suddenly we could appreciate the beauty and the cleanliness of the house, and we could relax and enjoy company.

Now when something is going on in your life and you are harbouring bitterness and offence, it becomes like this forgotten and unattended meat. It produces a horrid odour and harbours disgusting magots. When you are coddling offense, bitterness and unforgiveness, people can sense something is "off" about you. A certain gloominess will be hanging around you like that bad odour.

We must watch over our spirit, soul and body and guard against offense. No matter how someone has crossed the line with you, or even lodged a serious lawsuit against you. The way you handle this is using the wisdom of God towards solutions. Every battle is not about swinging your sword or knowing how to shoot, but to know when to use your weapons and when to be still. It is not about standing on the right to be offended for it is like forgetting to switch your fridge on and expecting to enjoy fresh food.

Part of keeping your heart pure is through self-examination. Man might think that he is only controlling himself, but there is always something controlling him as well. Those who are being controlled by the light of God, will always win while handling problems. You must understand that sometimes having opposition is okay. It is fine to disagree, but you must reflect and ask yourself why you disagreed. Maybe you have a point, but it can also guide you to go to avoid going into the wrong direction. It might redirect you to the right direction. You should self-examine ~ how can you do things better in the future? You cannot be learning the same lessons repeatedly. You must break through into a new horizon.

Whenever there is a night, there will always be a morning coming. What you plan for the morning, determines your day. Lay aside your offenses, empty yourself at each sunrise. Allow the Lord to fill you with love, joy, and wisdom. You need the right knowledge to apply you to be prosperous and successful. It is not just about keeping busy but knowing how and when to do things. It is about knowing when to fight, when to use your influence. But when you are being controlled by rage and unforgiveness, you might miss out the light and the way out. You may be led to personally engineer the protection of your spirit, keeping it from being corrupted or susception to greed or rage. You keep your inner voice innocent which leads you to the freedom of truth. Then you will produce health for your body.

Whatever offence you have experienced, always check why you were offended and why the person offended you. There are people who will never want peace with you or want your forgiveness or even ask forgiveness. When dealing with these people, fix your innermost being by saying "I forgive you". Sever that string that holds you to them. The Holy Spirit will guide you and give you strength to overcome if you ask Him. You will see His glory, goodness and peace start rising in you and the beauty of God will start manifesting in your eyes and your body language. This is when the Holy Spirit disconnects you from any kind of negativities and offenses. He will fill you with His knowledge and goodness.

Confessions and Meditations

Start saying good things about yourself. Do not curse yourself but bless yourself. By doing so, anxieties and depression will not take control of you. You are greater than that. You will give strength to your inner voice and to the truth you will confess, which is the Word of God. The reality of your situation might be real, the pain might be real, but you are not delusional. You cannot keep, nurture and imprison the pain. Emancipate yourself in boldness and courage to release your heart from self-inflicted pain and bondage.

Confess that there is a greater purpose on earth for you. Every single pain or situation you are going through, can receive new breath to cure you from viruses of anger. It clots your blood so that you're not living freely but have blockages in your veins. So, clean up your blood. Allow the saturation of healing in your blood through forgiving and letting go.

If there are certain figures in your life that have caused great damage to you, confess that your value and health is more important than the memory of the hurting past. Only you can truly take care of you.

Think about what God thinks of you. You are made in His image. There is so much more about you, and you have been given abilities to create wealth and significance in life. If what you have gone through has caused you to lose money, allow God's grace to work through the situation, delete the offense and restore everything you have lost.

Luke 6:37-38 (MSG):

"Don't pick on people, jump on their failures, criticize their faults—unless, of course, you want the same treatment. Don't condemn those who are down; that hardness can boomerang. Be easy on people; you'll find life a lot easier. Give away your life; you'll find life given back, but not merely given back—given back with bonus and blessing. Giving, not getting, is the way. Generosity begets generosity."

---- | | ----

Chapter 10

ENDURANCE TO LIVE OF-FENSE-FREE

TO endure is to know why you are passing through what you are experiencing. You must always be optimistic. There is nothing in this world that can be fixed when you give it over into the hands of Almighty God. But you need perseverance, patience, wisdom and prayer.

Sometimes, even with the right counsel and relationships, your endurance needs to prevail. That is why you need Godly people who will point you towards victory.

Do not allow stress and anxiety to control you but meditate on when you were happy. Remember when you had happy thoughts and you were enjoying life. Focus on times when you were thriving and loving moments. Do not even let small losses and frustrations disturb your progress.

Every time in life when I was disappointed by people, I thanked God for the contribution they made for the time being and then embraced the new road ahead with a merry spirit embracing the new without them. A joyful spirit brings healing into your body and mind. Your health will not suffer as you choose the path of gladness. The joy of the Lord is your strength (Neh. 8:10).

Proverbs 15:13 (NKJV):

"A merry heart makes a cheerful countenance, but by sorrow of the heart the spirit is broken."

Proverbs 17:22 (NKJV):

"A merry heart does good, like medicine, but a broken spirit dries the bones."

Maybe you lost a large sum of money. Only through patience and wise strategy will you be led back to restoration. You might be in the battle of sadness, limitations, and defeat. The situation might seem impossible, but pain can be used to create new ideas and innovation. It is at the lowest point of the wealthiest people's lives, when they reached the end of their rope, when they were bankrupt, when they rose from those ashes by developing the most innovative wealth of ideas. I have found they took time to think and innovate and invent and landed up being one of the wealthiest people in the world.

The comfort and convenience of wealth can sometimes steal creativity, but if you're in a situation where there's no way out, it's the residing Spirit of God who creates solutions and grants us dominion over the earth is our saving grace. Studying the scriptures, this dominion includes having the ability to multiply. We exercise abundance over the lack of resources, money and properties. As long as you're alive and your mind is active, you can decide to keep getting up in the morning as you grab hold of relevant scriptures to apply to the current situation you're facing.

You can stay positive and encouraged as you seek His kingdom first in all things. But you must genuinely believe that you can come out of the difficult situation you are in. God is the God of all flesh. So whatever fleshly challenges coming against you, you should stay at peace for He is greater than this. Why should you rejoice when you have unforgiving family, you lost your job, your spouse has left you or your plans have not worked out? If you can just recapture your future and restructure your spirit –you will be taken on the path of prosperity and not side with a "glass-half-empty" attitude.

When the Israelites approached the promised land, they sent spies to inspect what they were up against (Numbers 13:32-33). These men came back with fear-filled reports of the giants dominating the landscape. They came back with a description that the people were "like grasshoppers". By adopting a grasshopper mentality, you are telling yourself that you are stuck. But Joshua defied this mentality. He was a senior man at the time, but he had the strength of a twenty-year-old because He continuously strengthened Himself through the presence of God. He wanted to conquer the mountains at a ripe age.

God is giving us the ability to overcome the mountain of offense. In the Name of the Lord, we can receive supernatural power to overcome an impossible situation. You can come out of offence having greater blessings than before. Face it with a victory mentality, a winning mindset, in the time of hardship. Begin to see the light at the end of the tunnel, not the trouble at the outcome. Before you overcome, you must reprogram the victory in your mind. You are only waiting for the favourable results to be embraced.

Faith, The Command of Your Imagination

When you're surrounded by debts or a situation where there is no way out, it is more important to start changing your perception, perspective and your imagination.

This needs to be a priority over spending time working on a game plan. Start imagining the promises of God concerning wealth and riches. Imagination is a powerful force, but you must know how to use it for a good outcome.

In Genesis 11 we see the account of the building of the tower of Babel – all because people became so obsessed with building, they imagined that "reaching the heavens" was a reality. God knew that this imagination had a corrupt motive and so He had to put an end to their plans by supernaturally confusing their languages and displacing them.

What if you used your imagination to live unselfishly, to serve the Lord, to love your family, to make lives better and be generous to those who need help? You would be receiving the agreement and favour of heaven with these dreams.

If you owe a million-dollars, imagine yourself receiving ten-million dollars. If you have broken relationships in your marriage or family, imagine yourself being reconciled and healed by the power of God's love and confess your belief in God's power in prayer. If you have someone who refuses to forgive you and is harbouring resentment, imagine them being convicted by the Holy Spirit to repent for their sin and receiving the healing touch of the Lord. Your faith is the command of imagination. You must understand this.

Job 22:28 (NKJV):

"You will also declare a thing, and it will be established for you; So light will shine on your ways."

Hebrews 11:6 (NKJV):

"But without faith it is impossible to please Him, for he who comes to God must believe that He is, and that He is a

rewarder of those who diligently seek Him."

Inner Repair

Do not let the inner issue make you sink. Usually, it is not about who will get you out of your situation, the answer is within yourself. Conquer your own doubts and unbelief. God and His angels will always help you for He promised to always be with you.

You need to make the decision not to die here. When the Apostle Paul was expected to die when a snake hidden in the firewood bit him, he simply shook it off and the poison was unable to harm him (Acts 28:5). It opened an opportunity for people to have faith in God and he could lead many to repentance and salvation.

David encouraged himself in the Lord when the enemy captured his wives and children (1 Samuel 30:6). The men fighting with him were threatening to stone him because he had kept the families aside, yet exposed, and so the enemy took advantage of that. He could have accepted defeat through offense, anger and fear, but he went into the secret place and sought the Lord. With an encouraged heart, David could make favourable decisions for the future of his life and nation.

You are to value yourself and to conquer your worries and anxieties in the heat of situations. You need to pick yourself up and rise above all the things threatening to pull you down.

The Power of Discipline

As mentioned in previous chapters about being a soldier of Christ, I encourage you to continue abiding in the Lord and He will grant you the fruit of self-control (Galatians 5:22). Walking dependent upon the Holy Spirit leads you away from the lusts of the flesh.

Being disciplined enables you towards success in many things, but especially to not become a slave of anger and emotions.

There's a story of a boy who did not know who his parents were. When he was older, het got to meet his parents, but he was not treated as part of the family. He was treated as an intruder and would not be given his due privileges.

As he received the gift of dependence upon God, he defaulted to being thankful instead of angry or resentful. Everything he had and everything he had become was seen as a gift from the Lord. Therefore, he received a high level of being disciplined by having control of his passions and emotions. He kept choosing the blessing of the peace of God. He kept dreaming, even when people looked down on him or abused him.

This boy makes me think of Joseph from the Bible. He was separated from his father by the betrayal of his brothers. All because he had the favour of God, and that threatened their position in the family. Joseph had dreams and ambitions. These were a threat to his brothers.

We must understand that God has destined us for royalty – in His plan there is always success. Your destiny is in God and so start going after the dream He has given. He is enough and so are you. When the restorative blessings start coming in your life, you will attract new friendships and you will be able to give into their lives. Leaders and kings will be attracted to you and your gift. When they get to know you, they will realise they were also attracted to God inside you and get to meet Him too.

Isaiah 60 prophesies how the anointed of God will "arise and shine" and how they attract the wealth of the nations and kings. We only need to believe that the Lord has lofty and extravagant plans for His beloved ones.

Kingship Counters Offense

To overcome offence, you must understand God's principle about rulership and dominion.

Genesis 1:26 (NKJV):

"Then God said, "Let Us make man in Our image, according to Our likeness; let them have dominion..."

Here we clearly see that God intended rulership, management, and stewardship for each person. As Creator and Nurturer of His creation, we are designed in that same blessing. It is good to have ambition, to have a goal and a vision in your life and to reach the top of your game. But not everything good is God. Most want to become a king of some sphere or people and desire to live the lifestyle of the rich, famous and the royal. But being a king is not all about having money or resources but having the noble values that are embedded in the character to maintain dominion. Godly values make you worthy of having the capacity of rulership and establishing a "throne" or kingdom.

There may be as many titles and thrones as there are unfinished assignments, projects and companies that need to be stewarded. Without the inner dynamic of divine kingdom vision, you do not carry the energy and capacity of a king for that company or property. The same goes for managing relationships in friendships, family and in marriage.

Matthew 6:33 (MSG):

"Steep your life in God-reality, God-initiative, God-provisions. Don't worry about missing out. You'll find all your everyday human concerns will be met."

There's something about people who have been trained to be kings by the abiding Holy Spirit. He can send them anywhere and their rulership will trump any circumstance or challenge. Just like a lion roaming through various environments, he will still dominate as the "king of the jungle" no matter where he is. Some people who attempt or pretend to be lions are only mere dogs; no matter what they do and how hard they imagine themselves to be top dogs in a lion's world. One of the reasons why people remain dogs is that their inner world is not configured to the values of the nobility of spiritual kingship.

The wicked ways of man are described in Psalm 36:1-4 which contrast the royal, preserving ways of the Lord and His servants as described in verses 5-6:

> *"Your mercy, O Lord, is in the heavens; Your faithfulness reaches to the clouds, Your righteousness is like the great mountains; Your judgments are a great deep; O Lord, You preserve man and beast."*

Where there is oppression, depression and intimidation, there is no preservation, we note this when dogs are attempting rulership. But when the righteous rule under the governance of God, the earth rejoices (Prov. 29:2). Righteous rulers who live under the command of love, understand the vital need to live humbly before God, take authority and dominion to bring order and healing. As this scripture so graciously expounds, the loving submission to the mercy, faithfulness, righteousness, and humility of God opens the way to forsake offense and unforgiveness and brings restoration to an environment, industry or social structure.

Righteous rulers live above the limitations that offense bring and the restrictions that unforgiveness forms. The rulership of God within a life allows the overcoming power of the Lord to already reign in and through them in every sphere of life. They already have all of heaven to their disposal. Godliness is within them – they are His kings and priests to rule in this dimension of the universe, continuing and expanding what Jesus started.

Revelation 5:10 (AMPC):

"And You have made them a kingdom (royal race) and priests to our God, and they shall reign [as kings] over the earth!"

The Righteous Rule of Freedom from Offence

The righteous rule of King Jesus emanating through a life does not dominate with anger, manipulation, and control. It is not self-righteous and independent to enforce the will but lives *through* the will of the King.

Many times, we have festering and undealt with anger about a situation, but it spills over into our work, business, personal and spiritual life. Only the Holy Spirit can bring His peace and healing to emotions and body. We need to keep a twenty-four-hour check on the roots of anger in our daily connection with God so we may live stress-free.

Ephesians 4:26 (AMP):

"When angry, do not sin; do not ever let your wrath (your exasperation, your fury or indignation) last until the sun goes down."

Living offense free is living with a consistent, hopeful prayerful heart beyond the habit of introspection and selfishness. It is living from the heart of Jesus, seeing His kingdom come, His will to be done each day in every life, situation or circumstance (Matt. 6:10). The vision and blueprint of heaven is a reality mindset, allowing all that is said and done to become manifest on earth.

The King's kings do not allow their soul-realm to be lead with unsubmitted will and emotions nor limited intellect but is constantly tapped into the mind of

Christ through the inner intuition and conscience of the Holy Spirit. The glorious, intimate presence of Jesus brings the joy of a light but firm connection and an easy friendship (Matt. 11:28). It is a phenomenal, supernatural existence that is unburdened, guided, lead and nurtured in pastures green and to waters quiet (Psalm 23). Even though life is not exempt from the temporal walk in a broken world with hurt, pain, disappointments and loss, His presence grants the grace-filled capacity to give and create life in all seasons and spheres of life. It brings about a life that is testimony of the mystery of metamorphosis and how ashes can become beauty.

A person walking with the King becomes His eternal kingdom representative where there is uncompromised dependence upon the Holy Spirit. Everything the Father and Jesus represents lies within his or her consistent consciousness. There is an abiding peace of being sheltered by the Most High and counselled by the Good Shepherd (John 10) Who brings forth a life that is tenaciously life-giving and more than abundant (John 10:10). This submission to His leadership of life allows the growth of true purpose and optimal functionality filled with loving freedom and creativity.

Since kings have allowed The King's reign, His sovereignty and principles bring that inner security to always navigate life successfully. There is a sense of belief in the King's words that we are invincible and always part of a glorious solution. Since the love of the King has brought hearts and minds beyond themselves, the power of that love is always working to bring a redemption of the human nature. They find the transcendent grace to always be extending a hand towards others, despite the risk of it being bitten. The love of God keeps kings connected to this power to not only become a conqueror but *more* than a conqueror as they have learnt to conquer their own flesh first.

Creating Your Future By Deleting Offense

Since we were created in the image of The Creator, we were born for creativity. Offense can be a hindrance to creativity because creativity is tapping into the mind of the divine and bringing immaterial things into materialisation. Simply, making the invisible visible.

Ideas which are God's ideas will help the world operate better. For example, social media was an idea to connect a community, but now it has developed to such a degree, it is an instrument to connect the entire world.

Every time I spend time with God and allow His whispers through His Word to keep my heart pure from anything defiling or hurting me, I am living in His perfect intent. This is the key to be living free from grudges, offenses and unforgiveness.

Purekonect is a social media platform – an idea from God for people to be able to communicate apart from the limitations and risks that the most popular platforms have evolved into. It is set apart in that there is a pure motive for people to simply connect without the distractions and temptations of adverts and diverting interests. I dream to develop this platform into one of the greatest in the world.

A healed and whole heart is a free heart, a life unlimited and unfettered from inner wounding. As I was once seeking the Lord, He spoke to me about my value and how I should see myself through His eyes. He already views me as prominent, successful and accomplished. The world might think highly of someone famous, but does the Lord view them favourably? I am His beloved son and therefore, He will withhold nothing to sustain my intimate connection with Him, in addition, to provide and to equip me for the destiny He has planned for me.

Because of the salvation plan of Jesus and His redemptive work in me by the Holy Spirit, I am His delight and masterpiece. Having a divine connection with the King of Kings is our greatest wealth and accomplishment.

"Thus says the Lord: Let not the wise and skilful person glory and boast in his wisdom and skill; let not the mighty and powerful person glory and boast in his strength and power; let not the person who is rich [in physical gratification and earthly wealth] glory and boast in his [temporal satisfactions and earthly] riches;

But let him who glories glory in this: that he understands and knows Me [personally and practically, directly discerning and recognizing My character], that I am the Lord, Who practices loving-kindness, judgment, and righteousness in the earth, for in these things I delight, says the Lord."

Jeremiah 9:23 (AMPC)

---- | | ----